EVANGELINE

Fair was she to behold, that maiden of seventeen summers.

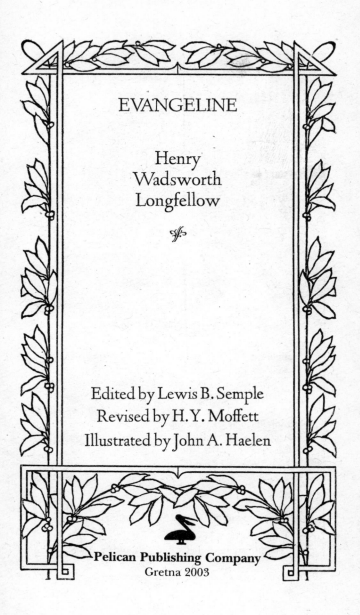

EVANGELINE

Henry Wadsworth Longfellow

Edited by Lewis B. Semple
Revised by H. Y. Moffett
Illustrated by John A. Haelen

Pelican Publishing Company
Gretna 2003

Set up and electrotyped. Published September, 1900.
Revised edition with illustrations published September, 1929.
Reprinted September, 1929; October, 1929; June, 1931.

First Pelican Pouch edition, April 1999
Second printing, February 2003

Library of Congress Cataloging-in-Publication Data

Longfellow, Henry Wadsworth, 1807-1882.
  Evangeline / Henry Wadsworth Longfellow ; edited by
    Lewis B.
  Semple ; revised by H.Y. Moffett ; illustrated by John A.
    Haelen. —1st Pelican pouch ed.
    p. cm.
  ISBN 1-56554-474-9 (alk. paper)
  1. Acadians—Legends—Poetry.   I. Semple, Lewis B.   II.
    Moffett, H. Y.   III. Title.
PS2263.A1 1999
811'.3—dc21   98-50342
                                                      CIP

Printed in the United States of America

Published by Pelican Publishing Company, Inc.
1000 Burmaster Street, Gretna, Louisiana 70053

FOREWORD

Against all odds, a universal Acadian symbol

I live in "the land of Evangeline". Well, to be fair: one of the two "lands of Evangeline", the Northern one. Two parts of the world, separated by thousands of miles, owe some of their identity to this strange Evangeline, whose Odyssey you hold in your hands. More than 300 separate editions in several languages, illustrated by more than 160 visual artists would be quite enough to qualify a literary creation for the Arts Hall of Fame. With two "lands" in her name, the heroine of our poem becomes a real star.

If you travel from Yarmouth, brought there by the very fast Cat, or if you rent a car after landing at Halifax International Airport, to visit the Canadian province of Nova Scotia, you may well drive down road 101 towards the small cities of Windsor and Wolfville. You cannot miss the panels along that well-known tourist highway, labeled "Evangeline trail". Inevitably, you will see indications to reach the historical site of Grand-Pré. You will probably join those thousands of tourists who come from everywhere in North America and in Europe, in a form of pilgrimage to a place that has nearly become an Acadian shrine. Some will go as far as leaving roses at the foot of the statue of Evangeline, who has become one of the most universal symbols of the unique identity of the Acadian community.

In a year when, for the second time in their history, Acadians from all over the world meet in a World Congress in the Acadiana parishes of Louisiana, Evangeline, who followed herself the path of exile to Louisiana, will not lose any of her appeal as a universal Acadian symbol...

Longfellow's narrative poem, one of the first long American narrative poems, was originally published in 1847. The year 1997 was marked in many places by activities celebrating its 150th anniversary, and the Acadian magazine, Ven d'Est, chose for its cover the title "The thousand faces of Evangeline". I doubt that many people would celebrate on such a large scale the birth of its creator in 1807, or his death in 1882. While Longfellow's fame has been waning with time, Evangeline's appeal has been growing, although for very different reasons, and in diverse environments. She was published and illustrated, drawn or painted on canvas. She was sculpted in wood or in stone on church pediments. She can be found on a stained glass window inside the cathedral at Moncton, New Brunswick. You can buy her on hooked rugs in Chéticamp. Her presence is such that some started believing long ago that she had been a creature of blood and flesh sometime in the past. In Grand-Pré, late 19th-century tourists already wanted to find her bones...while in St. Martinville, Louisiana, some were convinced those precious relics were there. In Grand-Pré at least, there might have been an element of truth to the presence of Acadian relics. Under the present park, lies one the numerous Acadian burial places in the region.

Anyone who has traveled to countries like Italy would not be surprised by the celebration of relics, after waiting in line before the shrine of Saint Anthony of Padua. There is only one problem with having Evangeline as an Acadian saint: it would be hard to find any relics...except Longfellow's manuscripts, carefully written in pencil at night, and copied in ink the next day.

While we often hear that Evangeline has no historically attested existence, as is indeed true, it would be hard to conclude this from the many uses her name is daily put to in the Maritimes or in Louisiana even today. In November 1998, I have heard her name repeatedly in a round table on Acadian economy, in connection with tourism in particular: Acadians, like Cajuns—although in a less colorful way—are considered excellent candidates for "cultural tourism" in the 21st century. In January 1999, I read a long editorial in the weekly Le Courrier where it was once again repeated that our Evangeline was not a "true" Acadian. On the Website of the new Acadian Webmagazine CapAcadie, I read her name several times. January 1999 marked a new opening of an exhibition, organized originally in Moncton for the 150th anniversary of the poem, devoted to her many faces—literary, musical, visual—at the Nova Scotia Museum at Halifax, a travelling exhibition that will come to Wolfville (and Grand Pré) this Summer. Newspaper reports and radio have devoted a fair amount of space and time broadcasts in early January to a debate that rages at the French Acadian university in Moncton and involves Evangeline. New Brunswick visual artist Roméo Savoie, who illustrated in stark expressionist and conceptual fashion the "Eve" section of the name Evangeline, Eve-Angel-Line, in 1997, faces "politically correct" criticism of the way he depicted Eve's particular fate. During a two-month period, it is not a bad track record. How many others, during the same time, have encountered Evangeline somewhere? Countless others, no doubt...

True Acadienne or not, there is obviously no denying the continued presence in the Acadian milieu—both North and South—of this "imaginary" creature! A little more than 150 years after its birth, the nostalgic and romantic image created by H.W.Longfellow still serves as a powerful symbol for an Acadian community which is very much alive despite the odds it had to overcome in the last 200 years. The original message was meant clearly for the American public of the mid-19th century. It grew considerably through foreign editions in English, in Britain, Scotland, and Ireland in particular. It was amplified in French by its main French-Canadian translator, Pamphile Lemay, who basically rewrote the poem to suit the French-Canadian context of the late 1800s and his own literary tastes—one of the few cases in history where the translator can readily be considered "co-author" of his translation!

The literary heroine whom Longfellow created from reports by Connolly and Hawthorne of tragic events that befell the Acadian community in 1755 and the following years has become a universal figure, revered or criticized, but impossible to ignore. Her name became a powerful symbol of Acadian identity, individual or collective. In Acadian parishes in Louisiana, where our heroine had first looked for her beloved Gabriel—only to find him, according to a Louisiana version, married to another woman—Evangeline was used as a brand name. It immediately identified the owner of the business as a Cajun, while French had almost become illegal following the end of the War between the States.

This universal Acadienne is not only a symbol for Acadians. Canada's national newsmagazine Maclean's, published in Toronto, offered us in July 1998 a list of the 100 most important Canadians in the history of the country. Among the 10 major hero and heroines of Canada, Evangeline came in second! She was in good company, between the ancient governor-general, diplomat and hero of the First World War Georges Vanier, and Canadian hockey player by excellence, the «Rocket» Maurice Richard. There was, however, a slight distinction between them: Georges Vanier had been a historical celebrity, Maurice Richard was a hockey legend, but very much alive, while our Evangeline was still a fictional celebrity. Curiously, she was not the only one: in 10th place on the same list, we could find another famous creation from a writers' mind, Anne of Green Gables. Despite this, some remain convinced that Canadians lack imagination...

Surprising Evangeline! Born from the pen of a New Englander who admired above all European romantic poetry, she has become a Canadian heroine while her people, the Acadians, were in North America well before Canada—and especially the present Canadian federation—ever existed. She has become an icon of Acadie, under the pen and brush of artists that hardly knew Acadie and even less Acadians. She's been depicted as a New England girl, a Scot, a British lady, a Pilgrim girl, a milkmaid, in costumes from Normandy—all inaccurate by far, and usually set in a romantic and idealized series of settings that had little to do with the actual situation of Acadians. At that time, in the 1850s, they lived in small communities, marginal in a British colonial world ruled by English-speaking Maritimers, facing economic exploitation and political and social problems which would have required the realistic vision of Émile Zola or Charles Dickens to be accurately described, rather than Longfellow's sentimental poetry.

In spite of all, she is still there, this Evangeline of a thousand faces, and you hold a new face of her with this volume.

Even her worst critics find a positive element in the fact that Evangeline is a woman: after all, in the nineteenth century, were not most thinkers convinced that History was made by men, and especially by "great" men? Until recently, the importance of women in history, from major events to the history of private and daily events, was too easily forgotten. Evangeline, the virgin from Grand-Pré, pulled from its shores and its orchards right before her marriage to see her father die and lose her betrothed, does not hesitate to roam throughout all of known America in her quest. This shows stamina, to say the least. Does she not then devote her life to a noble endeavor, by caring for the sick and the poor? A company of Christmas products made her their Angel of mercy...

In this poem based on the tragic fate of an exiled people, men do not have the main, nor the most beautiful role. Colonial and British soldiers are saddled with the low and largely immoral task to deport innocent civilians. Are they not the prototype of many others soldiers, the world over, who will try to justify any "crime against humanity" by claiming that they "just followed orders"? Longfellow's poem, although it is not an essay on politics, may be one of the first mass products in literature to make us think how inhuman it is to uproot a community and destroy it. In a long poem about the Displaced Persons of the Second World War, called Le Grand Dérangement (1955) French poet Paul Gilson takes Evangeline and the Acadian exiles as one of the symbols that corresponds best to the difficult situation facing the many victims of Hitlerism. The expression "Le Grand Dérangement" is used by all Acadians and Cajuns to refer to the destruction of their country, Acadie, in the middle of the 18th century.

To this day, even the most biased defenders of the old British colonial system have not been able to justify why civilians had to be deported, killed, doomed to die in prison ships and far-away jails, when there was no military threat looming, and France and England were not even officially at war (a situation they were used to anyway). Despite the fact that several poems by Longfellow, from The Village Blacksmith to The Wreck of the Hesperus, have been such consistent fare for schoolchildren all over North America that he's been labeled a "textbook poet", there was a strong anti-Evangeline feeling in some parts of the Canada at the turn of the century. After all, did the poem not imply serious wrongdoing by a British Empire that was then considered the embodiment of all virtues? Had it not been written by a Yankee, making the offense worse? The province of British Columbia even pulled it out of the school system, and numerous "historians" across Canada, mostly amateur, selecting documents from freshly opened archives, decided to prove that Acadians were in fact "terrorists", responsible for their own fate.

On the other side, largely due to French translations but particularly the three versions of the poem by Pamphile Lemay, the poem took on a deeply nationalistic tone, mixed with nostalgia, and a definite "Evangeline cult" started, first in Quebec, then in Acadie, where it took on much more than a literary dimension. It became part of Acadian culture—even, to some extent, a cornerstone of it.

Most other men in the poem do not have a much more remarkable role than the soldiers. Father Félicien (drawn, according to some, from a real priest by the name of Félix Pain) is without a doubt a noble figure: after all, neither in New England nor in French Canada, would it have been correct to give a negative depiction of a man of God. In somewhat the same way, Basil the Blacksmith incarnates the age-old role of a blacksmith in being a central power in a community. The notary, on the other hand, incarnates without a doubt the situation of a man torn between two masters, ready to compromise with the British at all costs. And Gabriel, who becomes a fur trapper in the poem by Longfellow, looks quite dull when compared with Evangeline. In one Louisiana version of the poem, written by Felix Voorhies, he is cast in an even worse light. He forgets Evangeline, gets married and has many children while she continues to be faithful to her dream, and sinks into madness when she discovers he'll never be hers. Gabriel plays so much second fiddle to Evangeline, that William King Baker is the only one of the many authors who rewrote the poem to devote a book to him, Gabriel Lajeunesse, illustrated by Sophie Foy and published in London in 1922. 1 out 130: compared with Evangeline, Gabriel is a lightweight.

When you arrive in my land of Evangeline, you will easily discover that Longfellow was far from wrong when he asked

Where is the thatched-roofed village, the home of Acadian farmers
Men whose lives glided on like rivers that water the woodland...
Naught but tradition remains of the beautiful village of Grand-Pré...

There is, today, a village in Grand Pré, mostly residential, which has even been recognized as a historic district by the province of Nova Scotia. You will not, however, be able to see what Grand Pré might have looked like in Acadian times on the shores of the basin, with all the hustle and bustle of an active trading and agricultural center. Except for guides at the historic park, you will not hear a lot of French being spoken. In this region, the heart of old Acadie, notices and placenames are mostly in English. You may discover many French names here and there: Grand-Pré, Gaspereau, Pereau, Melanson...You may notice that today, little by little, a French life resumes here some its activities. Acadian life in the Maritimes is definitely not reduced to the nostalgia of a few peasants and a few fishermen. French schools, small French-speaking associations, bilingualism efforts by the Department of economic development and tourism, bilingual brochures of the federal government, small Acadian businesses are some elements by which you will know that the old Acadie, which shaped this territory through its dykes, although reduced to minority status, did not disappear.

Surprisingly, Longfellow's poem is not only one of the most successful literary works of the American 19th century, but one the first literary documents to have served as a source for cultural tourism, which is seen by so many today as a remedy for economic ills. In the stride of the poem, people travelling through the "lands of Evangeline" in the year 2000—like you—will have been preceded by innumerable tourists for more than a century! In 1909 already, the Dominion Atlantic Railroad company published a brochure for vacationers coming to Nova Scotia from the U.S. through Yarmouth. After going through regions in the Southwest of the province where some Acadians resettled after coming back from deportation, our guide takes us to Minas Basin and Grand

Pré, a land with "mystic" qualities. For writer, jeweler and poet J.F. Herbin, partly Acadian on his mother's side, "So long as Evangeline is read Grand Pré will be a Mecca for the tourist." It is hard not to think of Grand Pré and "The Land of Evangeline" as sacred ground...

In 1909, projects were started to connect the grand and tragic place that had become a symbol of the expulsion of the Acadians with Longfellow's poem as well as some memorial buildings. Visitors, yesterday as today, quickly feel a particular, overwhelming emotion here. We could apply to Grand Pré and the surrounding lands what Swiss travel writer Nicolas Bouvier tells about some unique sites elsewhere on our planet: "Some places are charged with a particular power. They look whole to us, seem to convey a message we might decipher, a spiritual harmony of form and color». French writer from Lorraine Maurice Barrès talked about "those unique places overflowing with soul". Most tourists will simply say: "It's beautiful". Some may, looking at the bronze bust of Longfellow, wonder why he never visited the place, relying instead only on descriptions and historical accounts, seeing woods and oak trees of Celtic fame where dykelands and French willows were so obvious.

There may be a reason. Primeval forests and oak trees are creations of nature, with no human hand intervening. Dykelands and French willows both mean that nature was tampered with, that the harmony, the peculiar beauty of the region, are not simply the work of some unbridled forces of nature, but point to the presence of the Acadian community that has shaped the environment we still live in today. The soul of this place is made also of the mix of cultures that has taken place there, from the Mik'maq presence to the current Canadian diversity. It is suffused with nostalgia, the romantic quality that Longfellow's languorous narrative poem is imbued with. Longfellow, in his romantic vision, wanted nature to remain while culture disappeared. His woods, non-existent on the site of Grand Pré, are transferred straight from German romanticism. Sadly for him, had he been at Grand Pré, he might have noticed that the primeval woods were not far at all, and were possibly considered by Acadians with some kind of awe...

When you enter the park at Grand Pré, you cannot miss Longfellow's presence any more than you can miss the well of Evangeline, the memorial church or the statue of our heroine. It may seem ironic that, through a twist of fate, an American poet who never set foot either in Grand Pré or on the shores of Bayou Tèche (where his Evangeline seems magically immune to mosquitoes and heat) has created an icon of Acadian identity that endures to this day, and has become so vital to Acadian consciousness that it took over, in our minds, from the real people who lived here, died of old age and were buried on this very spot, or were murdered, imprisoned, or expelled. Some may find disturbing that so much attention was bestowed upon an imaginary figure, ever since the poem was first published. Some, however, may feel that it is many ways marvelous to have created such a haunting figure that she still, despite the passing of time, embodies some of our hopes, and many of our fears.

Some English-Canadian writers fearing for the unity of the British empire and its Canadian branch tried desperately to prove, against all evidence, that Acadians had not really been civilian victims of a military abuse of power not dissimilar to what the news brings us today from places like Bosnia, Rwanda, or Kosovo. Others, on the contrary, followed in large numbers in the footsteps of Longfellow: the first volume of poems by Bliss Carman (1861-1929) was called Low Tide at Grand Pré, and included a poem by that title the romantic mood of which would not have disappointed Lamartine, Shelley, Chateaubriand or Longfellow. The message remains, made strikingly clear by the flow of water that Longfellow used so much to indicate the passing of time: days go by, rivers flow, people vanish, and yet nature remains, eternal. In any anthology of Canadian poetry from the 1890s to the 1940s you are likely to find short romantic poetry connecting the feeling of sadness about the passage of time and the landscape at Grand Pré. Poets are not alone, either. Poet, but mostly novelist and occasional writer of tourist brochures for the DAR, Charles G.D. Roberts (1860-1943) chose the region as landscape for much of his historical fiction, playing upon the dual appeal of nostalgia and a vision of Eden on earth, as in The Forge in the Forest:

Where the Five Rivers flow down to meet the swinging of the Minas tides, and the Great Cape of Blomidon bars out the storm and the fog, lies half a county of rich meadowlands and long-arcaded orchards. It is a deep-bosomed land, a land of fat cattle, of well-filled barns, of ample cheeses and strong cider; and a well-conditioned folk inhabit it. But behind the countenance of gladness and peace broods the memory of a vanished people...

There is little doubt that this large literary production in English about Grand Pré and its particular atmosphere finds its source in Evangeline, and to a lesser extent, in the novel about Acadian exiles that precedes it under the pen of Providence writer Catherine Reid Williams, with The Neutral French (1841). What never ceases to amaze me is how much is written today still from that inspiration: the latest, on my desk, being a manuscript by a Maine author called From Here to Avignon, an original remake of the Evangeline story in novel form.

In the 1950s, French poet Alain Bosquet compiled an anthology of American poetry. He considers Longfellow a rather dull poet, but even he has to admit to the musical quality of Longfellow's poetry. The most famous poet of his time—as he is sometimes known—may suffer from being too much of an academic, a member of the New England upper classes, a "textbook poet" and a sentimentalist in the eyes of many: he remains a master of music, a wizard with an uncanny ability to write poetry the form of which often stands the test of time more than its content. His unrhymed dactylic hexameters (in which each of the six stressed syllables is followed by one or two unstressed syllables) proved an original challenge to the 1847 public, and play a large part in the enduring appeal of the poem. Anyone who compares the original poem with translations in French, often contrived and forfeiting the original rhythm for more classical verse, knows how much the musical abilities of Longfellow are unmatched in his time, and possibly in ours. It is no surprise to find some of Longfellow's poems on "New Age" recordings these days.

It is, no doubt, through the translations in French and the

following adaptations of all kinds that Longfellow's poem has become an important element for Acadian culture, particularly at the turn of the 20th century, both North and South. Charles Brunel did the first translation in Paris in 1864. French-Canadian writer Charles Lévesque did the first adaptation in 1854. The best-known French translation was done, and redone three times, by Pamphile Lemay, a French-Canadian poet who translated several works from English. It is a fair assessment to say that, despite their impact, those translations are usually far from emulating the musical qualities, the original rhythm, and the subdued but powerful images present in Longfellow's text. The conclusion, in 1999, is that…another translation of Evangeline into French will be forthcoming some day. It may well coincide with another one of the many adaptations of the poem, which has been retold in prose, as operas (from Belgium to the United States), on jazz records, in comic strips (including one where Evangeline becomes a fighting nun), and as a play in Church Point, Nova Scotia, with a text in Acadian French as spoken today in the region.

Some Acadians resent the presence of Evangeline. Her image is viewed as old-fashioned and unrealistic. They criticize the fact that she is still considered as the main Acadian symbol, when the true Acadian reality at the time, and the present Acadian situation, are either ignored or seen through Longfellow's rosy glasses. Somehow, this non-native girl reminds them too much how little, for a long time, Acadians were able to talk about themselves, having to leave such a task to more "cultured" communities. Is this Acadian icon not due to an American who had based his knowledge on texts written by writers from England or from France? Were not the translators and adaptators, in most cases, French-Canadians from Quebec, with little actual knowledge of Acadians? Does it not unduly insist on misfortunes and sufferings of the past, when the real challenge for a community that survived and grew despite all odds, is to face the uncertain future all linguistic minorities face the world over?

There is no real answer to this well-founded question. As all writers know, nobody has any control over the success or the failure of a book or a movie. Some of Longfellow's most successful "moral" poems have fallen into oblivion long ago. Most translations of Evangeline never reached a large public. Most editions were not reprinted. Despite that, Evangeline endures. Acadians are not alone to have inherited, as their main collective myth, an image born outside their community: William Tell, the main hero of Switzerland, comes from an Icelandic legend, passed onto the Swiss by traders at some point in history. Joan of Arc, a symbol of France, was not French but from Lorraine, a neighboring country at the time, and the only image we have of her is a small drawing on a recently discovered wall in a small chapel.

Evangeline, like all symbols, inevitably draws irony as much as praise. Young Acadian artists and writers in New Brunswick in the 1970s and 1980s saw her mostly as a symbol of the past. Many of their mothers had worn the Evangeline costume, seen as part of the older generations. She was not modern. She did not wear miniskirts. A poster went as far as to undress Evangeline as a paper doll! Evangeline: myth or reality? asked poet Herménégilde Chiasson in a 1980 show. Seventeen years later, he painted the part «ANGE» of her name, including excerpts from Lemay's translation, probably answering his own question. Isn't a myth real in our minds?

French rewriting of the poem in many forms has been the work of numerous authors. Pamphile Lemay "translated" the poem three times. Maurice Trottier, a French New Englander, "translated" it twice. Maurice Achard, a French writer writing in Quebec, wrote several prose versions. Marguerite Michaud, an Acadian educator, wrote a version for young readers. Scores of novels followed the basic plot of the poem: in the work of Quebecois Napoléon Bourassa, Evangeline becomes Marie, Gabriel becomes Jacques. The Louisiana versions of the poem, along the lines of Voorhies' recreation, follows the fate of Emmeline Labiche and Louis Arceneaux—one of the many literary clones of the original Evangeline and Gabriel.

It took a poet to start the movement by which the park in Grand Pré was officially recognized as an important site for the Acadian community. The meaning went farther than Acadians again: descendants of the Acadian exiles number today at least three million, mostly in North America. From the first private efforts of J.F. Herbin in the early 1900s to reclaim the site of Grand Pré, this place has become a national historical Site of Canada, twinned recently with the Cajun Memorial of St. Martinville, in the southern Acadie, this distant, mysterious, exotic Louisiana...

If we were faithful to the true Acadian geography, we would write, as Acadian novelist Antonine Maillet in her novel Pelagie-la-Charrette, not "Grand Pré" (Great Meadow), but "la Grand'prée", a feminine word. In the region of Poitou, in central France, "une prée" means what the Dutch call a polder: fertile ground gained on rivers or on the sea. The particular landscape that has made Grand Pré and my Annapolis Valley one of the richest agricultural regions of the Maritime since 1630, is largely due to the work of Acadian settlers, continued and strengthened by successive immigrants, who sometimes became masters to the few remaining Acadians. Tourists of today, like 1909 travelers, look at, a landscape shaped by an original culture.

One did not find Cajuns in France in the 17th century. One found there Poitevins, Bretons, Savoyards, people from Burgundy, Briards and Basques: but there was no province called Acadie. In 1524, Verrazzano, an Italian captain, was the first to name Arcadie the Northeastern shores of North America. Arcadia was, in Greek mythology, a paradise, where beautiful people lived pleasant lives in perfect harmony with an abundant nature. Little by little, the name was transformed into Acadie, a region gradually defined as today's Maritime provinces of Canada, a small part of Quebec and a small part of Maine. From the 1630s, in this northern Acadie, a community forged its unique "Acadian" identity. Before all other groups of European origin, they were a distinct, largely republican, fiercely autonomous people, with a strong faith to support them. In the eyes of a Romantic poet, who was familiar with Moore's Ireland or Byron's attempts to fight for Greek independence, such qualities were a blessing: one of the tenets of romanticism is to support people in their fight for freedom. With a poem about Acadians, Longfellow adds to his creation of a true American mythology, which also includes his Hiawatha and threatened Indian communities.

The idea that Acadians come from Normandy is one of the important mistakes in the poem. Although Acadians came from several regions of France, most originate from the southern part of Poitou. French King Henri IV had brought to Poitou Dutch engineers to dam the marshes, creating the present landscape of the "Marais Poitevin" with its numerous canals. Aware of those techniques, just like the Dutch, Acadians were going to live close to waterways and seashores. The world of Evangeline follows rivers and streams, bayous and lakes. Longfellow, born in Maine, knew the seaside well, and expressed in some poems a feeling of nostalgia for his youth near the ocean. Our time of roads, airplanes and cyber relationships has perhaps forgotten this deep bond with the water that constituted Acadie as well as parts of New England. To evoke a people of the water, a fluid poetry, languorous, loaded of rivers and tide images, constitutes well the best choice.

You may, near Grand Pré, walk on the upturned soil of ancient dykes. At the other end of the Valley, near the Port-Royal of 1605, you will find the exact reproduction of a small Acadian house, and its garden, near a dyke, also known as aboiteau. On the site of Grand-Pré, you may meet a black-smith, who will make you think of Basil in the poem. Yonder, under the old willows, near the statue of Evangeline by Hébert father and son, do you see Evangeline herself, played by a young Acadian girl from the Baie Sainte-Marie, the "French shore"? Both blacksmith and Evangeline are employed today by the "Société de Développement de Grand Pré", giving Acadians some control over their most symbolic historical site.

In the 18th century, you might have been one these numerous French "from France" (as distinct from Acadians, Canadians, or Louisiana Creoles) who came to see what Acadie was like - and then wrote books in which they claimed an intimate knowledge of all things Acadian. In 1699, the Dièreville, a small aristocrat from Normandy, was one of the first to put in writing and publish in 1708 some affirmations that would stick to Acadians, and find their way into Evangeline. Acadians, according to Dièreville, liked to live peaceful lives, work as little as possible, have large families, and live in a community spirit from which theft, among other vices, was absent. They did not pay taxes, and lived following the rhythm of seasons. These Acadians looked truly like residents of the antique Arcadie: happy, carefree, provided for by an abundant nature. According to Dièreville, they were also mostly poor, easily frightened, and rather lazy. Longfellow, in the same vein, shows us a superstitious group, workers without great wealth, firm believers in a God-ordained order of things. Gabriel Lajeunesse, Evangeline's beau, hardly seems to have any ambition, but simply wishes to live close to nature.

Longfellow did probably not read Dièreville, whose text was in his time difficult to find. He read several volumes inspired by the same view, the history of l'abbé Raynal (published in France in 1770) and the Historical and Statistical Account of Nova Scotia (1829) of the strongly conservative Nova Scotia writer T.C. Haliburton, who based most of his description of Acadians on Raynal.

French writer Marcel Proust wrote that lost Edens are the only real ones. No wonder a paradise with only memories of a lost people, scattered all over American landscapes, were a tempting topic for a romantic poet. I think, however, that Longfellow, just like Catherine Williams, or even Hawthorne (who not only suggested an Acadian topic to Longfellow, but wrote himself on Acadian exiles in New England) had two desires, in addition inspiration that writers know well, and which does not answer to reason.

The first was to create narrative texts with American subjects. Apart from Indian legends, was there any topic that was more uniquely American, from the early ages, than the Acadian Odyssey? Woods and mists, however imaginary, added an aura of mystery to it. Longfellow, like Whittier, like Whitman on a different scale, is one of the founders, through Evangeline, of a North American consciousness in poetry. His translators and adapters will ensure that such a consciousness will be present among Acadians between 1890 and 1960 in particular, although more marked by a traditional, highly conservatism Catholicism, and by a strong French-Canadian nationalism.

The second, was to illustrate a human tragedy, answering the romantic longing for people who suffered. From the first lines, there is no doubt that the key to the poem is nostalgia, and a deep sympathy for the sufferings endured by Acadians. Longfellow, for all the outpour of nostalgia in his languorous verse, has not given an image of an Acadian community poor, wretched, and illiterate. Evangeline, like other Acadians, is dispossessed: she still holds her head high, from the North down the Mississippi, from the bayous to the mountains of the newly discovered West.

From the very beginnings of the French colony in Acadie, there was a school in Port Royal, not only for boys, but also for girls. It was, in France at the time, hard to imagine! There were in Acadie people literate enough to sign their name without problem, business people able and willing to trade in English as much as in French, administrators and notaries. Do we not find a notary public, the notary Leblanc, in the poem? There were actually, history tells us, Acadian women married to British officers...There were also, without a doubt, skilled craftsmen as well as peasants, fur traders as well as housewives tending kids and gardens, tellers of tales as much as fiddlers. The Acadian community was prosperous, despite its small numbers when compared to New England at the time: 10,000 people are small, compared to more of a million. Like New Englanders, they were deeply attached to their North-American environment. They had tasted a freedom that feudal Europe would not have granted them. They had developed strong community bonds for communal work, but remained strongly individualistic, their farms distant from one another. Their felt close to the Mik'maqs, so close their breeds would sometimes mix. They were astute business people. It is no wonder that a few Acadians, though badly treated by the British, were welcome by friends in New England; the father of Vénérande Robichaux, one of the first Acadian chroniclers of the Acadian reality through her letters, was able to find refuge in Cambridge and have her daughters educated there before they moved back to Quebec.

Those who consider Evangeline a symbol of abatement

and despair have probably not read a poem that constantly presents her as the very strong embodiment of what Longfellow considered feminine virtues—before feminism convinced us that women can do as well as men, if not better, in tasks that require earnestness and business acumen. Evangeline has to be strong. She has to be strong-willed. Throughout her ordeal, she never loses hope, and never loses sight of her goal: it is not only Gabriel, it is not only love, it is also the soul of l'Acadie, the sense of a community that may grow again given the chance. Evangeline is the embodiment of pride, just as Marianne is the embodiment of France. Did the latter's figure at the helm of a boat, as "The Great Return", not provide a powerful symbol to the fight against despair, during the dark hours when France was occupied and humiliated by the Nazis? Does it not evoke the image of Evangeline being rowed down the Mississippi? Her last choice, to become a Sister of Mercy, follows naturally in the footsteps of her fate: helping the whole of mankind is as noble a task as helping your own self, or your own community. Evangeline, although she may not make miracles, provides a soothing and healing power not dissimilar to the soothing and healing power of Longfellow's own verse to mend the wounds of time and separation.

Beyond her literary children, Evangeline has been put to many commercial uses for more than a century. Evangeline Motors, Evangeline Homes, Evangeline Realty, Evangeline Beach…As Acadian songstress Angèle Arsenault sang in the 1980s, she's definitely "Evangeline, Acadian Queen". In 1896 already, in her novel A Modern Evangeline, Carrie Jenkins Harris mocked the extensive use of Evangeline to name everything around Grand Pré. The visitor who comes from Louisiana is not surprised: there also, we find Évangelines everywhere. To quote Carl Brasseaux, companies using the name include "bakeries, streets, roads, service stations, hotels, paint stores, car dealers, dance halls and spicy sauces". Evangeline is present as much in oil research as in soft drinks. In New Brunswick, in 1908, the Ganong chocolate company considered that Evangeline corresponded well to the image they wanted to give their chocolate: a discreet sweetness that would linger in the mouth. I have, on my bookshelf, a bottle of Evangeline. Unfortunately empty...

In my region, however, the use of Evangeline is not a sign of Acadian identity. Wines from Pisiguid are not made by Acadians, and the Grand Pré motel has nothing particularly Acadian. As for Acadia university, if French has some place in it, it is first of all an anglophone institution that owes its origins to Baptists and Planters who have taken the place of Acadians, and its name to the incredible infatuation that has given the Maritimes, at the end of the 19th century in particular, a great number of "Acadian" names, probably because this region was viewed as the old Acadie—which it will always be.

I read Evangeline, when I was sixteen, as a primarily American poem. Luckily, I read it in the original, not in the ornate French translation—in classical rhymed verse—by Pamphile Lemay which turns out to be twice as long as the original! This poem is obviously an attempt at writing a long romantic narrative that will do for America what European romantic poets have done in older cultures. Longfellow, who spent a large part of his time translating from several languages, knew German romantic poets well. He had read Thomas Moore, the Irish author of the Elegies, whose attempt to create a rich musical texture in poetry had a clear influence on him. He certainly wanted to emulate, in some way, Goethe's poem Hermann and Dorothea (1797), and sought inspiration in the Swedish poet Tegner's The Saga of Frithiof (1820). A great admirer of Scandinavian writing, he translated Tegner and considered that he was the greatest Swedish poet.

Curiously, we remembered this Swedish source when, with Sten Eirik, in the early 1980s, we tried to put a show together for Grand Pré park, based on the story of Evangeline. There was in Longfellow's idyllic vision of Acadie elements coming from documents on Swedish peasants. This was also a period when romanticism, following on Jean-Jacques Rousseau's wonderfully wrong idea that men was naturally good (and that only civilization corrupted them) thought that peasants embodied all possible virtues. Being closer to nature, their whole beings exuded a deep harmony that was lost to people living in cities. Our project, which would have allied that Swedish vision to Acadian reality, was one of many that did not end up on stage. It allowed, however, Sten Eirik to write his Geline of Acadie, one of the many books from the poem that offers us an Acadian girl as a central character, in the stride of Yvonne of Lamourie: a sister to Evangeline by Charles G.D. Roberts.

Even to Acadian intellectuals who know how much Longfellow's Acadians are quite different from what Acadians really were, the appeal of Evangeline remains enduring. Like all symbols, like all myths, she somehow changes faces with time. The poem shows her getting old in four lines; you can see, walking around her statue in Grand Pré, that she gets older under your eyes. As New Brunswick filmmaker Léonard Forest wrote in the 1970s, "Evangeline cannot really wear miniskirts"; on the other hand, the magazine Le Forum at the university of Maine in Orono just reprinted a "Dear Evangeline" letter that I had "sent" her on the Internet two years ago. Get on the Web, and you'll see how many sites offer graphics, text, and additional material about the poem. Young Acadian women choose her to explain what l'Acadie of today consists of. Last but not least, her name will bring to your search scores of documents from the best-known newspaper that bore her name, the daily L'Évangéline published in Nova Scotia in the 1890s, before moving to Moncton until the 1970s.

When I first read Evangeline, no one tried to convince me, as was told to numerous youths in Maritime Acadian schools, that she was a historical figure. To me, the poem never looked like a document. I read in it a narrative of universal significance. It provided for a reversal of roles. Here were Ulysses and Penelope, but in reverse: here, Penelope had gone on an Odyssey to find her Ulysses. It was also Orpheus and Eurydice—but, here again, it was Eurydice who was searching for Orpheus through light and dark, only finding him on the threshold of another world. Through Evangeline, who shone brighter than all other heroines in Longfellow's works, the poet used the Acadian situation to reach a higher level, both in his art and his vision of the human soul. Needless to say, Evangeline was also Eve, and Gabriel the Adam of their soon-to-be-lost Garden of Eden. Her name, Bellefontaine, was a fountain of youth, while his—Lajeunesse—was youth eternal. This poem had also something of Romeo and Juliet: a Scottish illustration of 1863 gives Evangeline and her fiancé the very features and clothes of Romeo and Juliet. Having lost his first companion in 1835, the Cambridge writer had experienced the pain of mourning—which he would experience again, in more tragic circumstances, in 1861. Through his Evangeline, who allies beauty to fidelity, constancy to an indomitable spirit, Longfellow wanted to create a heroine equal to some heroines in European romantic literature. We even have a picture of his daughter, Alice, from 1858, in which she is dressed in a supposed Evangeline costume, probably based on costumes from Normandy that were for so long wrongly believed by American and English-Canadian writers to be the costume of Acadians...

Tegner or other romantic poets, German, English, or French, had found in the legends and folktales of their country the source of imaginary creatures that they fashioned. Longfellow uses a very American tale, related to him by Hawthorne, to build an American narrative. Although he may never have visited Grand Pré, he documented himself as well as he could, and remained faithful to its sources. Why did he not come to Minas Basin, he who knew Maine and had traveled to Europe? Catherine Williams, author of The Neutral French, had, with less financial means at her disposal, come to New Brunswick to meet some surviving Acadians, whom she called "neutrals". Why, when he had gone as far as Philadelphia, did Longfellow not travel to Louisiana, which he might have portrayed in more specific and realistic terms? We may never know, of course, but we can strongly suggest that his vision of Evangeline was so intense and so personal that he felt useless to be distracted with realism. Aware from childhood of the natural environment in Maine, he relied mainly for Acadians on documents he could find, read, and analyze as an academic, before transforming them through the creative process only poets know, where words become music, and the resulting vision goes way beyond simple meanings and descriptive passages.

Nobody ever implied that Longfellow had not done what academics do best, a thorough reading of available sources. The initial impetus was given one evening by his friends Connolly and Hawthorne from a story heard by an "Acadian exile", as Hawthorne called them in his own writings. Longfellow then read, took notes, organized a narrative. Gérard Dôle, to whom we owe a study on Acadian music, admits that both tunes Les Bourgeois de Castat and the Carillon de Dunkerque, that are referred to in the text, could well have been played in 18th century Acadie. He does, however, insist on the "poetic license" used by Longfellow in his choice of documents, however thorough he may have been in collecting it. He "uses musical elements gleaned in the course of his travels or in older music collections". In the same way, the poet invents a world of forests for the beginning of the poem that resembles more the Maine he knew from childhood than the dykelands of Grand'Prée. His Louisiana and the spaces of the American West are purely imaginary. He has Evangeline meeting her dying Gabriel in Philadelphia, not for specific historical reasons, but because he loved that city and dreamt about it as a setting for a scene in a narrative poem.

Did Longfellow, for some sections of the poem, draw his inspiration from lesser known, but still quite successful in her own right, Neutral French author Catherine Williams? While recognizing the greater literary abilities of the Cambridge poet, she was herself convinced that he had read her novel. The Neutral French, that we find in the libraries of several French-Canadian 19th-century writers, enjoyed a fair amount of success: Catherine Williams was invited in many places to meet with descendants of French neutrals, toured Catholic colleges despite the fact she was not a Catholic, and received a fair amount of money from the sales of that novel. It is sheer logic to think that Longfellow had, if not read it, at least been made aware of it. According to Ernest Martin, whole passages of the poem correspond to passages in the novel, although the plot is quite different in both. It would not be the first time Longfellow used another text for his inspiration: at least two other examples come to mind during his lifetime. Would this be sufficient to explain, though, why Evangeline survives and thrives as a literary figure and a symbol of Acadie, while Pauline in The Neutral French never reaches such status? The explanation through which the conservative views present in the poem suited the Catholic church in French Canada much better than the rather revolutionary views expressed by Mrs. Williams does not fare much better. The Quebec Catholic church tried to create numerous figures of martyrs and saints as models for French-Canadians that never went beyond a very limited recognition. Evangeline, who is no saint, from the first day she was made available to the public, escaped its author, made him famous, and survived many changes in taste, in American literature as much as in Acadian collective consciousness.

For Cajun writer Barry Jean Ancelet, if all Acadian women had remained virgins like Evangeline, faithful to a lost love, there would be neither Acadians nor Cajuns today! We know that 18th-century Acadian women married younger than their cousins in France, and had a number of children who, in the quiet and prosperous environment of Acadie, had a much better chance to survive than their European cousins. An only child in families, as Evangeline and Gabriel are supposed to be, is totally unrealistic for the times. Evangeline is clearly a symbol, and not a portrait of the typical Acadian woman, except in some indomitable moral qualities.

Here, she joins real Acadian women: those who, coming back to the Maritimes, or moving down to Louisiana, prodded their men to start rebuilding. She is, in a way, the ancestor of literary women in Antonine Maillet's works, from Maria à Gélas to Pélagie—strong women who always have the first role and lead the community.

While New England was beginning, in the 1850s, to change and become more heavily industrialized than it used to be, the imaginary idyll of Grand Pré, just like the great and rich spaces of an imagined Louisiana, formed a powerful contrast to the dangers of modern civilization. Not surprisingly, the two lands of Evangeline, the Annapolis Valley or the Acadiana of Southern Louisiana remain to this day primarily rural regions, easy prey for ecotourism or cultural tourism projects.

This poem has obviously given birth to a star. Whether we like Evangeline or not, whether we see in her the symbol of a miserable Acadie or the icon of Acadian courage and fortitude, this creature of words, whose name finally retained by Longfellow mixes Genesis and angels, has taken a dimension that exceeds by far its creator. Longfellow, who liked women, has created other women figures: Minnehaha, or Priscilla. But neither Minnehaha nor Priscilla have become myths.

When I hear Evangeline, I feel in Acadie. Even if I know that, today, surfing on the Web, I can find African-American Evangelines, or Filipino girls called Evangelina. Hearing Evangeline, I close my eyes and think of young girls who are proud of being selected as candidates for Evangeline in Acadian village festivals, just as during the Lafayette Mardi Gras Queen Evangeline and His Majesty Gabriel are elected, during of colorful ceremony.

Celebrations for the 100th anniversary of the poem had brought to Cambridge visitors from the whole world. Antoine Bernard, a Gaspé historian of the Acadian survival, noted in his journal, on November 30th, 1947 that the poem of Longfellow "had resurrected a whole nation". Nothing less! It certainly established an enduring bond between the poem and the Acadian people.

During 150th anniversary of the poem, in 1997, even the most modernist of artists rushed to take part in celebrations of Evangeline. A myth can be challenged, or debunked, yet it remains. The movie "Quest for Evangeline" by New Brunswick filmmaker Ginette Pellerin in 1994, quite cleverly, got Evangeline to speak for herself while looking for a new meaning to her existence. Nevertheless, it maintained the vision, disturbing to some, that Evangeline was doomed to remain a creature of the past. In an older movie, "La noce est pas finie" (the game is not over yet), singer Raymond Breault was kicked out of a village because he had criticized Evangeline. Maybe she never existed but in the mind of a poet, but she certainly acquired a new life in the hearts of ordinary Acadians...and Cajuns.

We should not forget that there is another "Land of Evangeline". Willows in Grand-Pré in the North find their match in oaks near bayou Tèche in Louisiana, where an Acadian memorial flame is now burning as an eternal thought. We can visit, in the heart of St. Martinville, the Evangeline oak. We can find the place where our heroine has supposedly been buried. In Longfellow's poem, her name was not the most typical Acadian name—although we can find some Bellefontaines in marriage records for Acadian families, the Girouards for instance. Gabriel's name, borrowed from a mountain man, definitely belonged to Lower Canada, the Quebec of today. When Judge Felix Voorhies (1830-1919) turned Evangeline Bellefontaine into Emmeline Labiche, claiming to possess family information passed on by ancestors from the village of St. Gabriel, he definitely took his heroine out of the realm of Acadian realism: there are no Acadian families called Labiche. He gave Gabriel, however, a stronger Acadian identity: he became Louis Arceneaux, and some texts about Evangeline, like René Babineau's, will claim that they found in a Pierre Arceneaux the "real" Gabriel— you can even visit his house.

This Louisiana story, that also knows several variants, differs on quite a few other points from the story created by Longfellow's imagination. Emmeline and her lover have been separated during the deportation of 1755. An orphan, Emmeline is adopted by the family of the widow Borda, who sees an angel in her, and therefore names her Evangeline. The family is exiled to Maryland—historically the only British colony to have welcomed deported Acadians at that time. The family decides, however, to join others who moved to Louisiana, a fairly realistic evocation: no Acadian exiles were exiled directly to Louisiana. There, Evangeline-Emmeline finds Louis, but discovers that he has changed. According to some, he married another woman with whom he has several children. According to others, as in Longfellow, Emmeline discovers Louis dying in a hospital where she works as a nurse. In the two cases, the poor Evangeline loses her sanity and dies, a haunting figure. Symbolic interpretations may abound: isn't Louis the symbol of Louis, King of France, who abandoned Louisiana? Evangeline, therefore, is a symbol of Acadie even stronger than Longfellow's: unless she is able to be herself, French and faithful to traditions, l'Acadie will disappear. What is lacking, though, is the haunting quality of Longfellow's verse…

Actress Dolores del Rio, a major star in Hollywood during the 1920s, lent her features to the sad and thoughtful statue of Emmeline Labiche, a Southern counterpart to the statue erected by Hébert, in Grand-Pré. In the North, the Dominion Atlantic Railway used the myth to promote tourism; in the South, according to a pamphlet of Southern Pacific Lines in 1929 (available today on the Web), Evangeline is buried behind the church of St. Martinville.

The feature film Evangeline by Edwin Carewe, shot in 1929, with a cast that included Dolorès del Rio, Roland Drew and Alec B. Francis, has been restored in the last few years. A major production from the last years of silent movies and the early years of sound, it presents us with an Acadie closer to Italy in a Shakespearian scenery that to the historical reality deciphered by collective memory and modern archaeology. All Acadians are handsome and, as in all literary clichés, their main activity seems to be to dance to the sound of fiddles while preparing huge meals. This perpetual fais-dodo probably embodied, for the filmmakers, a typically French "joie of vivre". This may be why Hollywood and other filmmakers have been so interested in Evangeline: An Acadian Elopement in 1907, then Evangeline in 1908, in 1911, in 1929. In the 1960s, Toronto businessman Harold Medjuck planned without success a feature film on the subject, but interest was waning; in the 1980s, Ginette Pellerin offered us a movie alternating between a documentary and historical fiction; and the recreation historical; in the 1990s, a movie may be shot from the show developed by Norman Godin and the theatre troupe "Les Araignées du boui-boui" at Church Point, Nova Scotia.

Movies are only part of the products created from Longfellow's heroine. In 1994, the Quebecois Marc Gagné composed a musical drama, "Evangeline and Gabriel". Other musical tributes include jazz tunes, romantic melodies like "My Angeleen", lyrical or surrealistic operas. The most famous Acadian opera songstress, Rose-Marie Landry, joined her voice to the more rock tones of Marie-Jo Thério to sing a new version of the song Evangeline, a traditional version of which was sung for a long time in all Acadian homes. Country singer Art Richard wrote his little tune too. Ethnographer Barbara LeBlanc devoted a whole Ph.D. thesis to Evangeline. Robert Viau, a literary historian, just devoted a study to the various faces of Evangeline. This is not perhaps the world infatuation for the film Titanic, but it is undeniably a cult.

Through all that, one forgets easily that Evangeline is first a poem, a work of art, which combines the recipe for success that can be found today in the movie Titanic: a tragic history, a history of love, a feminine celebrity that touches us deeply, a trip that serves as self-discovery. Had Longfellow, author of The Phantom Ship (a well-known legend on the shores of Acadie and New England) and The Secret of the Sea, created Evangeline in 1998, he might have done a movie, making crowds cry around the world. In its way, Evangeline, the ideal romantic heroine, is the ancestor of Rose in Titanic. Like Rose, she is tragically separated from her lover, in a tragedy both individual and collective. Individual, because real suffering cannot be shared; collective, because the deportation of Acadians, like the wreck of the Titanic, leave on history a powerful symbol for all mankind to ponder.

In the eyes of Robert Viau, "Evangeline represents the ideal of the woman of the nineteenth century: loyal, reserved, faithful, patient, deeply religious". At the same time, however, she moves into a realm of adventure, does not hesitate to cover considerable distances to find the one circumstances have wrenched from her. This dual aspect—submission to the order of things and fortitude in the revolt—has caused it to become a symbol for Acadian journalism. In Louisiana, at least four newspapers, including one in St. Martinville, have worn the colors of our small Acadienne. In northern Acadie, the longest-lasting newspaper, based in Nova Scotia at the end of the nineteenth century, before leaving for Moncton was called L'Évangéline until its disappearance in the 1980s. Called, between 1937 and 1944, La Voix d'Évangéline, it certainly claimed to be the voice of all Acadians. Educators' associations, chapters of the national society l'Assomption often chose Évangéline as a name.

Evangeline was a link, at a time when Southern and Northern Acadians did not know each other much, between Louisiana and the Maritimes. From 1930 to 1963, groups of young Cajun women from Louisiana came to the northern Acadie, the first with Dudley LeBlanc...dressed as Evangelines. In my northern Acadie, many young women, even today, are dressed as Evangelines...starting these days with Chantal Després, a young Baie-Sainte-Marie Acadian girl, who "plays" Evangeline in the park at Grand Pré.

After a visit to Grand Pré, you may travel to New Brunswick and visit the village near Bouctouche where another work of art, Antonine Maillet's La Sagouine, has given birth to a whole village, Le Village de la Sagouine. Once you have visited the country of the Sagouine and its Acadie of the late nineteenth century, you may cross the gigantic Confederation Bridge and visit, on Prince Edward Island, the house with green gables, that has given birth to the famous Anne, the small red-haired waif who was, like Evangeline, on the list of most famous Canadians.

Then, watching the blazing sun go down into the north Atlantic into which, on an April night, the real Titanic sank, you may notice that the three best-known tourist attractions in Canada's Maritime provinces have one element in common. The land of Evangeline, the country of La Sagouine, the island of Anne are all connected to images of women. From the girl, Anne, to the old lady—the Sagouine—through the eternally young Evangeline with her black curls and the light in her eyes. None of these images corresponds to a woman in flesh and bone. In all three cases, these artistic creations have all become myths, the deep truth of which allows us to discover deeper meanings in reality, and in ourselves.

While Louisiana, in 1999, lives both its Francofête—the birthday of its foundation—and the second Cajun World Congress, Evangeline is once again made available for all. She does not wear a miniskirt, but she has survived and has become richer over 150 years. Acadie, far from being a small groups of survivors, has become, in the North as well as in the South, a community that is increasingly conscious of its international connections. Like Basques or Celts, among other victims of centuries past, Acadians have today the opportunity to be present on the whole planet without renouncing their roots, to be modern without renouncing traditions. Quite to the contrary, it is by recognizing the importance of traditions that one can live on a human level the situation of a global economy and world markets. Is there not, in Evangeline herself, a meaning corresponding to this: being faithful to our own identity, while adapting to our surroundings?

Strangely, a coincidence brings Longfellow closer to Acadians in their mutual sense of the passing of time. The poet translated, among the many translations he authored, a short poem by Santa Tereza de Avila:

Let nothing disturb thee;
Nothing affright thee;
All things are passing...

We can almost hear Acadians on their way to exile, their feet in cold water, pushed and prodded by British soldiers and New England militias, singing a hymn that provides the background for the movie Les Années Noires by Herménégilde Chiasson:

Under the sky
All things are passing
Every thing changes
All things are passing...

All things are passing...but Evangeline endures. Acadians, against all odds, survived and thrive. The character of Evangeline embodies the feeling that you cannot kill the soul of a people, even when it had to go through what Elie Wiesel, Nobel Peace prizewinner and survivor of Auschwitz, calls "the tenth circle of hell". The image, that adds a circle to the hell in Dante, would have pleased Longfellow, translator of The Divine Comedy. It is the incarnation of the blackness, the violence, and the destructive rage that continues to afflict humankind. Evangeline is perhaps too idealistic: but shouldn't we, threatened by darkness, opt for the light?

Let yourself be absorbed, gradually, slowly, into the rhythm of this poem. Follow, in her American adventures, the light of Evangeline, which is also the soul of Acadie. Few might have suspected in 1847 to what an extent this poem was going to create ripples in American and Acadian imagination for centuries. Read the poem aloud, slowly, in the deepest voice you can muster. It was not made to be read with the eyes only. It was made to be heard, almost sung. Read it to yourself, to those whom you love. Let its rhythm grow into you, its images permeate you. It may not be historically accurate, but it has certainly the right pitch to touch us, move us, make us dream.

Against all odds, the daughter of Longfellow's imagination remains, and will be for many years, a universal Acadian symbol, if not an Acadian symbol for the whole planet.

Henri-Dominique Paratte

PREFACE

"EVANGELINE" has long been an almost essential part of the literary heritage of American youth, and rightly so. Narrative poetry is naturally more attractive to young people than other kinds; Longfellow is a master of the long metrical tale, and this poem represents his most successful effort in that field. It is a wholesome, touching story, cast in a form of lofty, solemn beauty. The tone is high, as always in Longfellow, and the pathos and sentiment have no kinship with either the morbid or the mawkish. With the technical objections of critics the teacher in a secondary school has no direct concern. The verse form will be found suitable to the mood, and the rich and abundant figures of speech should be appreciated and enjoyed, not dragged through the mire of formal analysis. Every teacher, of course, will teach the poem in his own way, according to his taste and personality. He will discover the need of giving attention to unfamiliar words and improving the vocabulary of the student by reference to the dictionary and by the study of synonyms. There will be a great deal of reading aloud, much of it by the teacher, who should not neglect thorough preparation for so great a privilege; there may be dramatization of selected scenes, reports on individual historical, biographical, and literary investigations, and occasional bits of writing on carefully limited topics. Since the average pupil will be ignorant of the literary qualities of such a classic, the teacher must help his class to gain adequate knowledge of background and setting, of characters and their development, of the means whereby characterization and description are made effective, and of the organization and progression of the narrative. The immediate aim should be pleasure and satisfaction. After these will follow emotional growth and intellectual culture.

H. Y. M.

CONTENTS

Introduction

	PAGE
Longfellow's Life and Works . .	xiii
The Acadians	xxxvii
The Metre of *Evangeline* . .	xlvii

Maps

Map to Part the First . . .	lii
Map to Part the Second . . .	liii

EVANGELINE

Prelude	3
Part the First	5
Part the Second	56
Notes	111

ix

ILLUSTRATIONS

PAGE

Fair was she to behold, that maiden of sev-
enteen summers. . . . *Frontispiece*

Close at her father's side was the gentle
Evangeline seated 19

Not far withdrawn from these, by the cider-
press and the beehives,
Michael the fiddler was placed . . . 35

While in despair on the shore Evangeline
stood with her father. . . . 47

Far down the Beautiful River, . . .
Floated a cumbrous boat, that was rowed by
Acadian boatmen 79

Whispered a gentle voice, in accents tender
and saintlike,
"Gabriel! O my beloved!" 107

INTRODUCTION

Longfellow's Life and Works

Henry Wadsworth Longfellow was born in Portland, Maine, in 1807. His mother's family had been represented in New England as far back as the settlement of Plymouth; indeed, it is asserted that the poet was telling secrets of his own ancestors when he related the love story of John Alden and the Puritan maiden Priscilla. His father, Stephen Longfellow, was a lawyer, an honor graduate of Harvard College, and a man highly regarded for his courtesy, his public spirit, and his integrity of character. Fortunately, he was also well to do; he had a good library in which the future poet could nourish his growing mind, and he believed in education.

The poem "My Lost Youth" indicates that the boy's early life was a happy one. At the age of fourteen he left Portland Academy and, with his brother Samuel, enrolled at Bowdoin College at Brunswick, a school of which his father was one of the trustees. In college Longfellow made a number of worthy friends, Na-

thaniel Hawthorne and Franklin Pierce, later
President of the United States, among them.
In a class of distinguished students he stood
high. He seems to have found mathematics
difficult, but he found great satisfaction in
reading Gray's *Odes,* Dr. Johnson's *Lives of
the Poets,* and the works of Chatterton. Not
only did he read such literature with zest, but
he liked to discuss it; his letters to his parents
contain many expressions of his critical opin-
ions and show that even better than reading
he loved writing. He found time, too, to com-
pose verses which were printed in newspapers
and a number of prose articles that gave him
something of a local reputation.

As the time of graduation approached, the
thoughts of the young man turned to the ques-
tion of a profession. In those days a college
graduate ordinarily turned to the ministry,
medicine, or the law. Stephen Longfellow had
planned that his son study for the bar. Henry
was willing to admit that he might possibly
endure being a lawyer; for medicine and theol-
ogy he had much respect but no inclination.
"The fact is," he says in a letter dated Decem-
ber 5, 1824, "I most eagerly aspire after future
eminence in literature; my whole soul burns
most ardently for it, and every earthly thought
centres in it. . . . Surely, there never was a
better opportunity offered for the exertion of

literary talent in our country than is now of-
fered." And the better to fit himself for this
kind of work, he proposed a year at Harvard,
to be spent in the study of history and litera-
ture and in considering his future. The father,
a practical man, doubted the wisdom of such a
plan. He pointed out to his son the necessity
of making a living and the practical impossi-
bility of doing so by means of purely literary
pursuits. Admitting that the life of a man of
letters might be an agreeable one, he explained
that "there was not enough wealth in the coun-
try to afford encouragement and patronage to
merely literary men."

The father was right. At this time no single
American had been able to maintain himself
by his pen. Bryant had struggled for years
as a lawyer and had spent the rest of his
days as a busy editor; in late life he made the
statement: "An experience of twenty-five years
has convinced me that poetry is an unprofitable
trade—nobody cares a fig for it." Poe had died
in miserable poverty. Our literature was just
dawning. The great mass of Americans were
too busy with the stern necessities of life to
give thought, much less money, to the cultiva-
tion of the higher pleasures of the intellect.

At this juncture, when it seemed that the
young aspirant to literary distinction would be
obliged to grapple with the law, a most for-

tunate circumstance arose. In emulation of
Harvard, the trustees of Bowdoin proposed to
found a professorship of Modern Languages.
One of their number, a Mr. Orr, had been so
favorably impressed with Longfellow's trans-
lations of some of the odes of Horace that he
proposed that the chair of Modern Languages
be offered to the young graduate. The accept-
ance of the offer was a matter of course. This
was exactly the opportunity that Longfellow
wanted. As a teacher he could carry on his
favorite studies; he could interest others in
things that interested him; above all, his
duties would afford him some leisure for lit-
erary work. It was suggested that he spend
three years abroad, gaining familiarity with
Spanish, Italian, and German, as well as im-
proving his knowledge of French, before as-
suming the new position. This great undertak-
ing the young man approached with confidence
and enthusiasm. In May 1826, Longfellow
sailed from New York, reaching Havre after a
pleasant voyage of a month. The next three
years are a record of sight-seeing, letter writ-
ing, and study. Within three weeks after his
arrival in France, we find him installed in a
boarding house in Paris, where the use of Eng-
lish by the seven American boarders was for-
bidden under a penalty of one *sou* a word. His
letters home speak much of the delight which

all the novel sights and experiences of Europe held for a young and enthusiastic observer. But they also indicate his realization of the seriousness of the duty which had brought him abroad. To his father he writes " . . . I had no idea that it was indeed so difficult to learn a language. If I had known before leaving home how hard a task I was undertaking, I should have shrunk."

After a time Longfellow left France and visited Spain, Italy, and Germany. A pleasant episode of his sojourn in Spain was an acquaintance with Washington Irving, who was then writing his *Life of Columbus*. The author of the *Sketch Book*, a volume that had been one of Longfellow's boyhood delights, was very kind to his young countryman and gave him letters of introduction to many distinguished men in the quarters of Europe into which he was later to travel. Longfellow was impressed by the sunny temper of the veteran man of letters, and also by the zeal and persistence of his literary toil, for Irving was customarily at his desk by six in the morning and labored faithfully and conscientiously at his huge task.

The influence of Irving may have been in part responsible for the fact that in May 1829, Longfellow writes from Germany, "I am writing a book—a kind of Sketch-Book of scenes in France, Spain, and Italy." This turned out to be his first important publication, *Outre-Mer*. Shortly after this date he was summoned home, and his first European sojourn was at an end.

In the fall of 1829, Longfellow took up his active academic duties at Bowdoin, with a salary of eight hundred dollars a year as professor and an additional hundred dollars for serving as librarian. His department was a new one. He himself was eager and full of the recent inspiration of his European studies. His youthfulness won the sympathy of the students, and there is abundant testimony to the pleasure they found in associating with one who could preserve the dignity of the professor and yet meet the students on their own plane. Nor was the work so difficult as to be burdensome. Though there were recitations, lectures, and examination, and though the young professor found that he had to translate and compile textbooks for the use of students, there was still some time for study and for original composition. This last was most important, for Longfellow had not forgotten his ambition for literary distinction.

Up to this time Longfellow's publications had been neither numerous nor important. Some prose papers had appeared in the *American Monthly Magazine* and in the *United States Literary Gazette*, and from his schoolboy days

he had written occasional verses for news-
papers. In 1831 the editor of the *North Amer-
ican Review* requested contributions, and for
years Longfellow's papers on European lan-
guages and literature appeared in that maga-
zine. The echo of a poem read at the meeting
of the Bowdoin chapter of Phi Beta Kappa, in
1832, reached Cambridge; and the author was
asked to repeat it there, and later to print it.
Apart from translations, his first really serious
publication was *Outre-Mer,* the "kind of
Sketch-Book" mentioned above, which was
brought out in 1835. In his journal he describes
it as "composed of descriptions, sketches of
character, tales illustrating manners and cus-
toms, and tales illustrating nothing in particu-
lar." The influence of Irving is clearly discern-
ible in this book. It was eagerly read at the
time, perhaps because European travel was not
so common then as it has since become, and
the impressions of an intelligent traveller, im-
mature though they were, were welcomed. It
was even more popular in England than in
America, so that the writer began to have
something of a reputation across the water.

In the year 1834 Bowdoin experienced re-
verses of fortune. Funds were low; the State
Legislature refused to make necessary appro-
priations; and Longfellow began to look else-
where for a position. Then fate smiled upon

him for a second time. George L. Ticknor, professor of modern languages at Harvard College, resigned, and, having been well impressed by the zeal and scholarship of the young Bowdoin professor, recommended Longfellow as his successor. The offer carried with it the privilege of a preliminary year or more of study abroad; and for a second time Longfellow embarked for Europe. This time he was not alone, for he had married Mary Storer Potter in 1831.

The second journey was made under much more favorable conditions than the first. Longfellow now had a reputation to assist him, largely because of the favorable opinion of *Outre-Mer*. During a stay of three weeks in the British Isles, he became acquainted with many persons of note, including Mr. and Mrs. Carlyle. The sojourn in England was delightful, and might have been prolonged had he not found it necessary to hasten to his study of German. He wished also to gain some acquaintance with the Scandinavian languages. Going first to Stockholm, he vigorously prosecuted his studies. Until December 1836, he divided his time chiefly between Switzerland and Germany, living for a while in the old university city of Heidelberg, where he found the best facilities for his studies in the German language and literature. In the autumn of 1835, during a trip to Holland, he experienced his first great sorrow, one that deeply influenced his life and work; for his wife fell ill, and in November she died at Rotterdam.

Harvard, which was the scene of Longfellow's activities from 1836 to 1854, was a far more attractive place than Bowdoin. The scholastic traditions were high; Ticknor, Longfellow's predecessor, was a man distinguished as teacher, scholar, and writer. On the other hand, Harvard had something to give in compensation. Cambridge was the centre of a group of men deeply interested in literary matters. Longfellow knew well the value of the privilege of associating with men of tastes similar to his own; before many years he had become the centre of a group of poets which are still called in the books the "Cambridge School." It was not long before both the college and the town discovered that the professor conferred upon them more honor than they had conferred upon him.

One cannot think of Longfellow without also thinking of the historic Craigie House, famous as Washington's headquarters during the siege of Boston, and since become one of our most sacred literary shrines. In 1836 the house was the property of Mrs. Craigie, an eccentric widow, who finally consented to receive the young professor as a roomer, after he had convinced her that he was not a student. Learning that he was the author of *Outre-Mer,* she assigned him as a special honor the room which had once been occupied by Washington. Here he prepared the lectures which his college duties required; here he made his translations and wrote his poems; and here he entertained his friends, Felton, professor of Greek, Charles Sumner, who lectured in the law school, the lawyers Hillard and Cleveland, Nathaniel Hawthorne, and other men of note. Henceforth, since Longfellow is now well launched into his literary career, we shall consider him as writer rather than professor, although he retained his professorship until 1854.

Outre-Mer is the literary fruit of the author's first sojourn in Europe; *Hyperion* is the literary fruit of the second. In the meantime his ideas had matured; his vision had clarified. As a result, the latter work has more consistency than the former; the sketches are bound together by means of a hero and a heroine, and the result rises almost to the dignity of a romance. To a certain extent *Hyperion* has an autobiographic value, the hero representing in some measure the author himself.

The same year that saw the publication of the romance (1839) was marked by the appearance of the first volume of poems—*The Voices of the Night,* which achieved immediate and gratifying popularity. In this volume

Longfellow inserted poems lately published in the magazines, such of his earlier verses as he thought worthy of preservation, and a number of translations. Among the original poems were such favorites as "A Psalm of Life," "Hymn to the Night," "The Light of Stars," "The Beleaguered City," and "Footsteps of Angels," the last being written in memory of his wife, and springing from deep personal feeling. The prevailing note of the *Voices* is one of gloom and sadness. There was also represented the didacticism or tendency to moralize that characterized much of Longfellow's work. Of this characteristic "A Psalm of Life" is typical. The writer was deeply serious in his view of human life and also deeply grounded in the principles of religion. And so it is natural, teacher that he was, that he should attempt to teach moral lessons in his poetry. The "Psalm of Life," proclaiming faithful performance of duty, the responsibility resting upon each human being for the welfare of his fellows, and the hope of immortality, found quick response in many hearts and was an inspiration to thousands of humble people in America and abroad. If the merit of poetry is to be measured by its result, surely "A Psalm of Life" belongs among the masterpieces. Modern readers may find it commonplace and "preachy"; but its effects were wholesome and wide-spread, and we must value it as the clearest expression of the author's philosophy of life.

The translations, all of them lyrical and some of them in the ballad form, were well done, and did much to bring to the American reader the spirit of German literature and thought. Incidentally, this work marked a step in the development of the poet, preparing him for his later treatment of original themes in poems of the ballad kind.

The volume was kindly received in the circles that Longfellow was most concerned about —his friends and the book-buyers. Nathaniel Hawthorne, Washington Allston, and N. P. Willis lauded them. Even Edgar Allen Poe, who had very sharply criticized some of Longfellow's work, expressed his admiration for "Hymn to the Night" and "The Beleaguered City." Hawthorne declared that he "had read the poems over and over again, and they grew upon him at every re-perusal." The first edition of nine hundred copies was exhausted within three weeks. The critics who attempted to belittle the poet's efforts, and who perhaps hoped to discourage him, failed of their purpose. Was ever author so indifferent to adverse criticism or so provokingly lenient toward the critic? A review that promised to be unfavorable was thrown into the waste basket; and its writer received a personal notice, like the following, in the poet's Journal: "He seems very angry. What an unhappy disposition he must have, to be so much annoyed." All the while, amid the press of college duties and the preparation of lectures, a new volume was being prepared.

In a letter to a friend, under date of January 2, 1840, Longfellow says: "I have broken ground in a new field; namely, ballads. . . . The *national ballad* is a virgin soil in New England; there are great materials." Among these materials which the poet used was the wreck of a number of ships near Gloucester, one of them a schooner named *Hesperus,* and also the discovery of a skeleton in armor, which associated itself in his mind with the Norse sagas that he had studied. And in 1841 was printed the second volume of poems, *Ballads and Other Poems,* containing "The Wreck of the Hesperus, "The Skeleton in Armor," "The Village Blacksmith," "The Rainy Day," and "Excelsior." Probably no other American writer has attempted the ballad with a greater degree of success. "The Wreck of the Hesperus" was in form and in spirit a fine imitation of the old English ballads; "The Skeleton in Armor" was vigorous and Norse in spirit; "The Village Blacksmith," in spite of the characteristic moralizing at the close, has long been a great favorite, and will continue to be as long

as there is left in the land a village black-
smith-shop and a village boy to stare round-
eyed at its wonders.

In the spring of 1842 Longfellow secured
leave of absence for six months. He was suf-
fering from nervous exhaustion, and a physi-
cian had recommended the baths and treat-
ments of Marienbad, Germany.

The question of the abolition of slavery was
agitating the country at this time. Charles
Sumner, one of Longfellow's closest friends,
took an active part in the movement, and was
destined to become a leader among the Aboli-
tionists within a few years. He was anxious
to secure the influence of Longfellow. But the
poet was not enthusiastic. He disliked all vio-
lent measures, and the remedies which some
were proposing seemed to him worse than the
evils against which they were directed. He was
opposed to slavery, but he hoped that the sys-
tem might be done away with by legislation
and by compromises that would do justice to
slave-owner as well as to slave. He declined
to join any group or to take part in any cru-
sade, but he did write several poems on the
subject while returning from his sojourn in
Germany, and after his return they were pub-
lished in a thirty-page pamphlet. These are
tender and pathetic, and rather romantic than
realistic. Though they caused bitter attacks to

be made upon him by some, others felt that he had not done justice to his subject. And indeed, when compared with the writings on slavery of men like Lowell and Whittier, Longfellow's verses are feeble and ineffectual. It requires stronger convictions than his to "poetize practical themes." Still, Whittier was so gratified to have Longfellow come out, even feebly, on the Abolition side, that he offered to have the author of "The Quadroon Girl" and "The Warning" nominated for Congress as candidate of the Liberty Party. But from such an honor as this the poet shrank. To Whittier he wrote: "At all times I shall rejoice in the progress of true liberty, and in freedom from slavery of all kinds; but I cannot for a moment think of entering the political arena. Partisan warfare becomes too violent, too vindictive, for my taste; and I should be found but a weak and unworthy champion in public debate."

College duties were resumed in 1843. Shortly after his return from Europe, the poet married Miss Frances Elizabeth Appleton, whom he had met in Europe. Longfellow's father-in-law purchased the Craigie House, Mrs. Craigie being now dead, and presented it to the couple. Longfellow was now permanently settled in the house he loved, and there he spent the remainder of his life.

To the year 1845 belong three popular po-
ems—"To a Child," "The Day Is Done," and
"The Old Clock on the Stairs." "Nuremberg"
is an artist's tribute to the artistic traditions of
the town; and "The Belfry of Bruges," which
gives its name to the volume, records an Amer-
ican's impression of a quaint Old World cus-
tom.

The publication, in 1847, of "Evangeline"
marks an epoch in the poet's career. Up to this
time he had confined himself to reflective lyrics
and ballads; he now turned to a longer form
—the tale in verse. The abundance of native
American material he had long been aware of.
More than once his thoughts had turned to the
early history of New England. At length a
chance conversation suggested a theme even
better suited to his genius. In his presence Mr.
H. L. Conolly, a clergyman, related to Haw-
thorne the story of the separation of two Aca-
dian lovers as a result of the expulsion of the
French settlers from Nova Scotia. Longfellow,
touched by the character of the heroine, said to
Hawthorne, "If you really do not want this in-
cident for a tale, let me have it for a poem."
And upon Hawthorne's consent, he determined
to set to work. This was the origin of "Evan-
geline," though at first the heroine was called
Gabrielle. Since only a slight historical back-
ground was needed, the poet did not take pains

to visit Nova Scotia or to dig deeply into the historical documents of the times; he used the authority nearest to his land, Haliburton's *History of Nova Scotia,* which quoted from the Abbé Reynal some highly-colored pictures of life in Grand-Pré.

"Evangeline" has been one of the most popular poems in American literature, particularly with young people. Critics may find fault— as many of them have done—with the hexameter which the poet chose to employ; they may regret the energy expended in the manufacture of comparisons; they may, if they please, deny to the poem all high literary value. But the people will continue to read, to blame the English, to sympathize with the heroine; and perhaps some of them, like Holmes, will leave upon the last leaf a little mark which tells more than words. The reason is clear: it is a story of love, ideal love, so simply told that the least imaginative can understand. There is no need of "putting oneself into a proper attitude" in order to comprehend it; all that is required is belief in "affection that hopes, and endures, and is patient."

The author never visited the scene of the story. Ideal surroundings were demanded, and ideal they are,—the broad, rich meadows, reclaimed from an angry sea by the toil of the settlers, theirs in a double sense; the hills—

Blomidon or any other—rising in the distance as if guarding the village; the quaint Normandy cottages and costumes of the peasants; and the venerable church casting its dim, religious light over all. Here the inhabitants lived a Utopian life. Modest desires and mutual helpfulness made the richest seem poor, and the poorest rich.

Of the characters that enter into the story Evangeline alone is vividly described. The others are clearly enough marked to be distinguished: Benedict, a prosperous farmer, well satisfied with the world and looking hopefully upon the future; Basil, the blacksmith, impetuous in judgment and in action, suspicious of the English, who had lately renewed their encroachments upon French territory; Father Felician, a model priest, the adviser of his people in temporal as well as spiritual matters; and, dimmest of all, Gabriel, the lover of Evangeline. Very charmingly is the home of Benedict pictured, with the young girl as central figure.

In the most beautiful season of the year, when Grand-Pré "lay as if new created in all the freshness of childhood"; when the homes of the villagers were gladdened by a successful harvest; when preparations had been made for the establishment of a new home in the community, came the mysterious summons of the English commander, and then the announcement of the cruel sentence. In the trying moments of the removal how much depends upon Evangeline, and how nobly she sustains her part! Thereafter her life is one of patient suffering, lighted by a single hope, tolerable because it is possible to forget self in the service of others. When at last the hope is realized, only to vanish away, the reaction is too great, and the strong nature breaks. There could be but this one ending. Any other would have dragged the story down to a very commonplace earth.

Kavanagh, a tale of life in a New England village, was not so successful. The rural scenes which make an admirable background for a poem are too tame for a romance, unless they are relieved by unusually clever characters. Longfellow's story lacks one element of the requisite combination. His friends spoke of it guardedly. There were other romances in the field, and opportunity was offered for comparison. But the poems entitled "By the Seaside" and "By the Fireside" (1850) aroused all the old enthusiasm. Most striking among these is "The Building of the Ship," the conclusion of which is the classic apostrophe of the Union. "Resignation" has all the intensity of the sorrow which called it forth.

The routine of college life was becoming

wearisome. The poet was now in easy circum-
stances. His books yielded a fair income. The
time had come when he could carry on his
literary work without the interruptions which
the duties of a professorship occasioned. He
therefore resigned (1854), and was succeeded
by James Russell Lowell.

In the Journal for June 2, 1854, is the en-
try: "I have at length hit upon a plan for a
poem on the American Indians, which seems to
me the right one, and the only. It is to weave
together their beautiful traditions into a whole.
I have hit upon a measure, too, which I think
the right and only one for such a theme." And
again, on the 28th: "Work at 'Manabozho';
or, as I think I shall call it, 'Hiawatha,'—that
being another name for the same personage."
The poem was completed and published in
1855. "Hiawatha" is certainly not an Amer-
ican epic, nor "the nearest approach to an
American epic," as has been asserted; nor can
it in any sense be compared to "Beówulf," as
one writer has ventured to compare it. There is
a vast difference between "Beówulf" and "Hia-
watha." The former is a national poem, the
expression of a people's traditions and ideals,
according to their own poetic instincts. "Hia-
watha" is a series of pictures of Indian life
drawn by a cultured American, who, for lit-
erary purposes, overlooks the real character of

the Indian; from a heterogeneous bundle of attributes and conditions abstracts one,—life in the open air,—and then represents him as a child of nature. We Americans might object to owning Hiawatha as our ideal. But no one will hesitate to acknowledge him as the idol of the American boy, the attractive personage with whom many happy hours have been spent. Nor can one deny the artistic claims of the apparently artless story—the swinging lines fitly bound together, the repetitions which echo in one's ears, the clear, pure atmosphere which the author's own personality has suffused about the whole. Seldom has it fallen to the lot of a writer to contribute so largely to the pleasure of youthful readers.

"The Courtship of Miles Standish," which has neither the interest nor the literary value of "Evangeline," appeared in 1858. The poem was well received, however, and encouraged the author to continue writing tales. The plan of "The Tales of a Wayside Inn," published between 1865 and 1874, was, of course, derived from Chaucer's "Canterbury Tales." The Red Horse in Sudbury takes the place of the Tabard in Southwark. The characters represent actual persons; whether or not they met at the Inn is another question. The stories were drawn from all sources: "Paul Revere's Ride" and "Lady Wentworth," from New England tradition; "The Saga of Olaf," from the Norse; "Charlemagne" and others, from French romance; one, "The Birds of Killingworth," is, it is asserted, the poet's own.

Of the remaining volumes—*Flower de Luce* (1867), *The Masque of Pandora* (1875), *Kéramos* (1878), *Ultima Thule* (1880), *In the Harbor* (posthumous, 1882)—little need be said. One poem has hardly attained the currency it deserves—"The Hanging of the Crane," a history of the home in panoramic pictures. But, as a whole, the latest efforts added little to the reputation of their author. American thought has undergone changes during the past sixty years; and from the movements that brought them about Longfellow remained stolidly aloof. In his latter days American literature was not the meagre growth he had found it in the beginning of the century. Perhaps it had risen above the standards he had set for himself.

In addition to the poems mentioned there are several plays: *The Spanish Student* (1843), *Judas Maccabœus* (1872, *Michael Angelo* (posthumous, 1883), and *Christus,* a trilogy including "The Divine Tragedy," "The Golden Legend," and "The New England Tragedies," the whole designed to show the course of Christianity. The drama has a fascination for all

poets, principally on account of its associations
with the past. But to one successful attempt at
play-writing there are many failures. The de-
mands of the classic drama, such as a great
poet must aim at, are so multifarious that few
can meet them.

Moreover, academic duties and interest in
literature in general called forth textbooks and
compendiums of various kinds. The transla-
tion of Dante's *Divine Comedy* was purely a
labor of love.

It was a busy life that ended on March 24,
1882. Though not so eventful as the lives of
great men usually are, it was none the less
sublime on that account. Its even course was
disturbed by the shocking death of Mrs. Long-
fellow, in 1861: her dress caught fire from a
match that had fallen lighted upon the floor,
and from the injuries received she died within
twenty-four hours. But the poet was not ac-
customed to parade his griefs before the pub-
lic His own theories urged resignation and
devotion to duty; and is it not his chief glory
that he was the best exponent of his theories?
The world readily recognizes the claims of sin-
cerity. It was to the man as well as to the
poet that two continents did honor. In 1868,
when he visited Europe for the fourth time,
the great English universities acknowledged his

services to literature by conferring upon him the highest academic degrees; the great men of England, France, and Germany saw in him the highest type of manhood. Nor were his own countrymen backward. Pilgrimages to Cambridge became the fashion. But the most significant of all is the well-known tribute of the children of Cambridge to the author of "The Village Blacksmith."

And how stands it with his poetry? There is no need of denying natural limitations. He himself conceded them when he said, "With me all deep feelings are silent ones." The masterpieces of literature owe their origin to deep feelings that are not silent. Longfellow was thus restricted to the expression of common emotions; yet for that very reason he reached a larger circle of readers than a greater intensity could have hoped to reach. And so, while his poems may lack a certain force which we expect to find in verse of the highest order, they nevertheless belong among

"The pleasant books, that silently among
    Our household treasures take familiar places,
And are to us as if a living tongue
    Spake from the printed leaves or pictured faces."[1]

---

[1] "The Seaside and the Fireside." Dedication.

THE ACADIANS[1]

AFTER the discovery of America it became a custom for the monarchs of Europe, especially those of England and France, to grant to such of their subjects as wished to undertake the enterprise, the right to colonize certain portions of the New World. These districts were always described in vague terms; in fact, the grantors themselves did not know what they were giving. In this way it happened that the two peoples frequently came to regard themselves each as the sole possessor of the same stretch of territory. For instance, in 1579 Queen Elizabeth granted to Sir Humphrey Gilbert a patent "for the discovering, or occupying, and peopling such remote, heathen, and barbarous countries, as were not actually possessed by any Christian People." Acting under this grant Sir Humphrey took possession of Newfoundland. Similarly certain Frenchmen, with equal powers from their sovereign, reached and attempted to colonize what is now Canada. They named their land, with no well defined limits, Nova Scotia.

The peninsula which we call Nova Scotia was discovered by Sebastian Cabot, in the English

[1] Haliburton's *History of Nova Scotia*; Smith's *Acadia*; Hannay's *History of Acadia*; Murdock's *History of Nova Scotia*; Gayarré's *History of Louisiana*.

service. Its settlement, however, is due to the French. The first attempt to colonize it was made by the Marquis de la Roche, in 1598. The Marquis was forced by unfavorable conditions to return to France, leaving the settlers to get along as best they might. They probably perished. More successful was the attempt of De Monts, who was made governor-general of the province by Henry IV in 1603. Two years later De Monts planted the first permanent French colony in America, at Port Royal, in what he called Acadia. From this time the growth of the settlement was rapid. But the names Nova Scotia and Acadia were used indiscriminately in the documents; and in subsequent treaties neither party was slow to take advantage of the confusion arising from this fact.

The English and the French had been enemies for centuries in the Old World, and it was only to be expected that their quarrels should be carried on by their representatives in the New. The English were constantly encroaching upon what the French regarded as their exclusive territory. For one hundred and fifty years (1605-1750) Nova Scotia, or Acadia, passed back and forth like a tennis ball. By the treaty of Breda (1667) England was to give up all claim to Acadia. But in the course of Queen Anne's War, Port Royal was taken by English and colonial troops. Its name was changed to Annapolis, in honor of the Queen, and encouragement was given to the inhabitants of Massachusetts colony to settle there. Under the terms of the treaty of Utrecht (1713) the natives were to hold their lands subject to the crown of England and were to be protected in the exercise of their religion —Roman Catholic. The natives, in consequence of these conditions, were known henceforth as Neutrals.

For many years the English did not succeed in making a flourishing settlement in Acadia. Finally, in 1749, the matter was taken up seriously: they disliked to see so fertile a district given over to the French without making an effort to get possession of it. In that year it was resolved to send out a colony, and, in order to secure settlers of the right kind, farms were to be granted to all who would undertake to improve them. Lord Cornwallis was made governor. In June he and his settlers arrived in Chebucto Bay, on the southern coast and, after exploring to find a suitable place for a town, founded Halifax, named after Lord Halifax, who had taken a lively interest in the project.

This move made the question of ownership of the peninsula a matter of some importance. The English and the French were now living in close proximity. The former were bent upon securing a firm footing in the land. The French were equally determined to prevent such a misfortune. Hence arose the troubles which ensued in the expulsion of the Acadians. The French asserted that the English were interlopers, and had no right to attempt settlement without permission previously obtained; because the Acadia ceded to them by the treaty of Utrecht was not the Acadia that Lord Cornwallis had invaded with his army of colonists. The English, on the other hand, maintained their right by reference to that treaty, and further insisted that the French had forfeited its privileges by hindering the new settlers and by inciting the Indians to war against them. Here was a serious misunderstanding. It was decided to refer the case to commissioners of both the mother countries. Of course the conference came to no conclusion.

Meanwhile, in the province discontent was rife. Lord Cornwallis summoned the Neutrals to take the oath of allegiance to his sovereign, and to promise assistance in case of war with the Indians or others, under penalty of losing their possessions. The French objected to the promise of assistance on the ground that the Indians would resent it, and requested the privilege of disposing of their possessions and leaving the country. To this Cornwallis rejoined that according to the treaty of Utrecht they were to leave, if at all, within one year, and that the right of withdrawing had expired by limitation. Conditions at this time were not favorable to a peaceable termination of the matter.

The outbreak of the French and Indian War, in 1754, brought the affair to a crisis. It now became a question of supremacy. In 1755 a determined effort was to be made to dislodge the French from their strongholds. The most important of these was Beau Sejour, in the district now called Cumberland. An expedition set out under Lieutenant-Colonel Monckton, with Lieutenant-Colonel John Winslow, appointed by Governor Shirley, of Massachusetts Bay Colony, in charge of colonial troops. The fortress was easily reduced. Winslow discovered, or professed to have discovered, that the Neutrals had been actively engaged in the defence of the fort. What was to be done with the offenders, who, according to the terms of the treaty of Utrecht, were traitors? After careful deliberation the commanders decided that the best course was to transport and disperse them among the British colonies, in the hope that the example of the loyal subjects of England might in time make Englishmen out of them. Accordingly, the following proclamation was issued: "To the inhabitants of the district of Grand-Pré, Minas, River Canard, &c.: as well ancient, as young men and lads."

"Whereas his Excellency the Governor, has in-
structed us of his late resolution, respecting
the matter proposed to the inhabitants, and
has ordered us to communicate the same in
person, his Excellency, being desirous that each
of them shall be fully satisfied of his Majes-
ty's intentions, which he has also ordered us
to communicate to you, such as they have been
given to him; We therefore order and strictly
enjoin, by these presents, all of the inhabitants,
as well of the above District, as of all the other
Districts, both old men and young men, as
well as all the lads of ten years of age, to at-
tend the Church at Grand-Pré, on Friday the
fifth instant, at three of the clock in the after-
noon, that we may impart to them what we are
ordered to communicate to them; declaring
that no excuse will be admitted, on any pre-
tence whatever, on pain of forfeiting goods and
chattels, in default of real estate.—Given at
Grand-Pré, 2d September, 1755, and 29th year
of his Majesty's Reign.

JOHN WINSLOW."

In response to this summons four hundred
and eighteen men assembled in the church.
They found themselves prisoners there; for, say
the historians, "even the church had been con-
verted into an arsenal." Colonel Winslow told
them that, in consequence of their abuse of the
indulgence shown them by the Crown, the au-
thorities had decided upon rigorous measures:
"their lands, tenements, cattle of all kinds, and
live stock of all sorts were forfeited to the king,

with all other their effects, saving money and household goods, and they themselves to be removed from the Province."

The surprise of the Acadians was complete. The colonel had cleverly worded his proclamation so as to give no clew to the character of the message he was to deliver. Escape was impossible, for the church was surrounded by soldiers. But the news quickly spread. Those who could escaped to the woods. They were not safe even there. The country was laid waste, houses were burned, and the more obstinate were reached by threatening the lives of their friends. On the 10th of September, 1755, more than a thousand persons, "the whole male population of the district of Minas," were drawn up in lines, to be driven upon the transports. The women and children were loaded on boats as fast as boats could be provided. As if to deprive the exiles of even the hope of return, their homes were burned while the transports were still in sight of land. The method of removal necessarily led to the separation of families, and thus deprived many of the unfortunates of the consolation the dearest associations of life might have afforded. They were taken to different provinces, and, if the truth must be told, were not very kindly received, except in Louisiana. For instance, a gentleman of Philadelphia, upon their arrival in Pennsyl-

vania, is said to have breathed a prayer that
"God might be pleased to grant success against
all copper-colored cannibals and French sav-
ages, equally cruel and perfidious in their
natures." In Louisiana, where kindred speech
won for the exiles the good-will of the colonists,
farming implements were furnished them at the
expense of the government, and they were per-
mitted to settle along the Mississippi between
the German Coast and Baton Rouge, a district
which came to be called the Acadian Coast.

Remonstrances were sent to the king, with-
out avail. One from the exiles in Pennsylvania
recites at length the hardships undergone at
home and abroad, and gives the experience of
René Leblanc, named in the poem, as an in-
stance: "He was seized, confined, and brought
away from the rest of the people, and his fam-
ily, consisting of twenty children and about one
hundred and fifty grandchildren, were scattered
in different Colonies, so that he was put on
shore at New York, with only his wife and two
youngest children, in an infirm state of health,
from whence he joined three more of his chil-
dren at Philadelphia, where he died without
any more notice being taken of him than of any
of us, notwithstanding his many years labour
and deep suffering for your Majesty's service."

Half the romance of the expulsion would be
lost without the Abbé Reynal's account of life

in the district of Minas. The people were industrious and, by constructing dikes, made the rich soil of the lowlands yield fifteen or twenty for one. The community supplied all its own wants; if any of the inhabitants desired luxuries, they could be procured by barter in Annapolis or Louisburg. Money was not needed. "Even the small quantity of gold and silver which had been introduced into the Colony did not inspire that activity in which consists its real value. There was seldom cause, either civil or criminal, of importance enough to be carried before the Court of Judicature, established at Annapolis. Whatever little differences arose from time to time among them were amicably adjusted by their elders. All their public acts were drawn by their pastors, who had likewise the keeping of their wills; for which, and their religious services, the inhabitants paid a twenty-seventh part of their harvest, which was always sufficient to afford more means than there were objects of generosity. Real misery was wholly unknown, and benevolence anticipated the demands of poverty. Every misfortune was relieved, as it were, before it could be felt, without ostentation on the one hand, and without meanness on the other. It was, in short, a society of brethren; every individual of which was equally ready to give and to receive what he thought the common right of mankind. . . .

As soon as a young man arrived at the proper age, the community built him a house, broke up the lands about it, and supplied him with all the necessaries of life for a twelvemonth. There he received the partner whom he had chosen, and who brought him her portion in flocks."

Too much credence should not be given to this account. One must remember that a Frenchman is speaking of Frenchmen who received a wrong at the hands of Englishmen; and that the narrator wishes to make the wrong appear as a great crime. The Acadians were certainly not faultless. Their interests were united with those of France; and their dislike of the English doubtless led them to take great risks in times when the fortunes of war might have turned the scale to the side of France as easily as to that of England. It was but natural that the English should retaliate when the opportunity came. Perhaps retaliation upon the whole people was unjust when only a few may have been at fault. The opinions of the historians are divided. One says that the lands of the Acadians were unusually fertile and the English coveted them; hence the expulsion. Another asserts that the Acadians might have remained if they had been willing to renew their oath of allegiance; that the refusal to do so was naturally, or at least not unnaturally, construed as an act of hostility. Whatever our judgment as to the historical facts may be, we may still feel the poetic charm and the tender pathos of Longfellow's poem.

THE METRE OF "EVANGELINE"

The metre in which "Evangeline" is written is called dactylic hexameter. Each verse contains six feet (hence the name hexameter). In the normal verse each foot except the last consists of an accented followed by two unaccented syllables (dactyl). The last foot has one accented and one unaccented syllable (trochee). If we represent accented and unaccented syllables by the letters a and u respectively, the structure of the normal verse is as follows:—

auu | *auu* | *auu* | *auu* | *auu* | *au*
This is the | forest pri-|meval. The | murmuring | pines and the | hemlocks.
Naught | but tra-|dition re-|mains of the | beautiful | village of | Grand-Pré.
Yet under | Benedict's | roof hospi-|tality | seemed more a-|bundant.
Touched were their | hearts at her | story, and | warmest and | friendliest | welcome.

As a succession of perfectly regular verses would prove monotonous, substitutions are frequently made, usually a trochee for a dactyl. Such a substitution may be made in any foot:

Strongly | built were the | houses, with | *frames of* | oak and of | hemlock.

Waste are those | *pleasant* | farms, and the | farmers for-|ever de-|parted.
Blomidon | rose and the | *forest* | old, and a-|loft on the | mountains.
Shone on her | face and en-|circled her | *form, when* | after con-|fession.
Into this | wonderful | land, at the | base of the | *Ozark* | Mountains.

A trochee is not often found in the fifth foot.

Frequently a verse contains more than one substituted foot:

Men whose | lives glided | *on like* | rivers that | water the | woodlands.
List to a | *Tale of* | *Love in* | Acadie, | home of the | happy.
Distant, se-|*cluded,* | *still, the* | *little* | village of | Grand-Pré.
Stand like | *harpers* | *hoar, with* | *beards that* | rest on their | bosoms.
Not in | *word a-*|lone, but in | *deed, to* | love one an-|other.

Monotony is further relieved by varying the position of the pauses. Obviously, pauses must be made in so long a verse, and their occurrence in any fixed place would give the reader an unpleasant jolt. The rhythmical pause may or may not be indicated by punctuation. In the examples that follow, *double, single,* and *half* strokes are intended to give a clew to the length of the pause.

There disorder prevailed, | and the tumult and
    stir | of embarking.||
Busily plied the freighted boats; | and in the con-
    fusion |
Wives were torn from their husbands, | and
    mothers, | too late, | saw their children   570
Left on the land, | extending their arms, with
    wildest entreaties.||
So | unto separate ships | were Basil and Gabriel
    carried, |
While | in despair | on the shore | Evangeline stood
    with her father.||
Half the task was not done | when the sun went
    down, and the twilight
Deepened and darkened around; | and in haste the
    refluent ocean   575
Fled away from the shore, | and left the line of the
    sandbeach
Covered with waifs of the tide, | with kelp and the
    slippery sea-weed.||
Farther back | in the midst of the household goods
    and the wagons, |
Like to a gypsy camp, | or a leaguer after a battle, |
All escape cut off by the sea, | and the sentinels
    near them, | 580
Lay | encamped for the night | the homeless
    Acadian farmers.

It will be noticed that the linking of verses
together has much to do with oral reading.
Verse structure and sentence structure may
correspond: ll. 171, 382, 509, 568, 624, 863,
etc. In such a case the sentence is usually a
topic sentence. But as a rule the sentence is

carried on from one verse to another, and this necessitates pauses of varying length at the end of the lines. For instance, ll. 569 and 570 are not so closely connected as are ll. 570 and 571: the prepositional phrase in l. 569 would be followed by a pause even in prose; the word *left*, l. 571, cannot be so separated from the group immediately preceding it. Notice ll. 574-5, 578-9. Further illustrations will be found in ll. 53-4, 83-4, 100-1, 137-8, 270-1, 561-2, 565-6.

The scansion of the line offers few difficulties. In general, a safe rule to follow is, accent the first syllable and the rest will take care of itself. The student may be aided by the device of beating out several lines to some familiar air in waltz time.

Although Longfellow was not the first to use the English hexameter, he did more than any other to establish it among our poetic forms, and, consequently, came in for some harsh criticism. The argument is briefly as follows: in Latin and Greek the principle of verse is quantity, in English it is accent; the classic hexameter invariably ends with two long syllables (spondee), exactly equivalent in time to the dactyl, and the same combination may be substituted for the dactyl in certain other positions in the verse; in English the spondee must be represented by the trochee; the classic hexameter cannot, therefore, be reproduced in

English. Occasionally the effect of the spondee may be suggested, when two words having equal or nearly equal sentence stress are brought together: ll. 47, 166, 185, 274, 308, 345, etc. But such occurrences are rare. Still it is hardly worth while to argue the case; Longfellow adopted the measure, and the poems clothed in it cannot be annihilated by a technical objection. John Forster who, like many other critics, could not reconcile himself to the use of the hexameter in English poetry, wrote: "You have done more with it than any other writer." In so far as "Evangeline" is concerned, the lingering lines harmonize with the solemn and melancholy tone of the story.

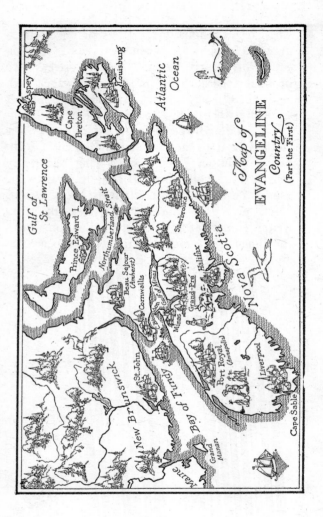

Map of
EVANGELINE
Country
(Part the First)

Atlantic
Ocean

Gulf of
St Lawrence

Aspey

Louisburg

Cape
Breton

Prince Edward I.

Northumberland Strait

Beau Sejour
(Amherst)

Cornwallis

Sherbrooke

Nova Scotia

Halifax

Grand Pre

Basin of Minas

Minas

Port Royal
(Annapolis)

Liverpool

Cape Sable

New Brunswick

St.John

Bay of Fundy

Grand Manan

Maine

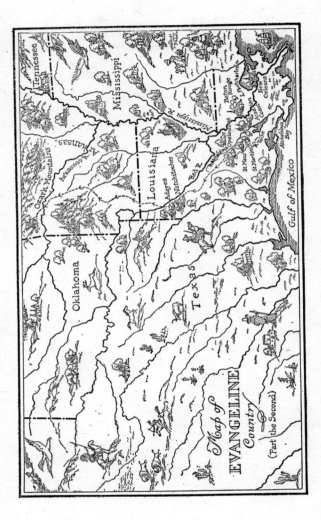

Map of
EVANGELINE
Country
(Part the Second)

EVANGELINE

EVANGELINE

PRELUDE

THIS is the forest primeval.° The murmuring
    pines and the hemlocks,
Bearded with moss, and in garments green, in-
    distinct in the twilight,
Stand like Druids of eld,° with voices sad and
    prophetic,
Stand like harpers° hoar, with beards that rest
    on their bosoms.
Loud from its rocky caverns, the deep-voiced
    neighboring ocean   5
Speaks, and in accents disconsolate answers the
    wail of the forest.

  This is the forest primeval; but where are
    the hearts that beneath it
Leaped like the roe,° when he hears in the
    woodland the voice of the huntsman?
Where is the thatch-roofed village, the home
    of Acadian farmers,—
Men whose lives glided on like rivers that
    water the woodlands,   10
Darkened° by shadows of earth, but reflecting
    an image of heaven?

Waste are those pleasant farms, and the farm-
ers forever departed!
Scattered like dust and leaves, when the mighty
blasts of October
Seize them, and whirl them aloft, and sprinkle
them far o'er the ocean.
Naught but tradition remains of the beautiful
village of Grand-Pré.°   15

Ye who believe in affection that hopes, and
endures, and is patient,
Ye who believe in the beauty and strength of
woman's devotion,
List to the mournful tradition still sung by
the pines of the forest;
List to a Tale of Love in Acadie,° home of the
happy.

PART THE FIRST

I

In the Acadian land, on the shores of the Basin
    of Minas,°   20
Distant, secluded, still, the little village of
    Grand-Pré
Lay in the fruitful valley. Vast meadows
    stretched to the eastward,
Giving the village its name, and pasture to
    flocks without number.
Dikes, that the hands of the farmers had raised
    with labor incessant,
Shut out the turbulent tides; but at stated
    seasons the flood-gates   25
Opened, and welcomed the sea to wander at
    will o'er the meadows.
West and south there were fields of flax, and
    orchards and cornfields,
Spreading afar and unfenced o'er the plain;
    and away to the northward
Blomidon° rose, and the forests old, and aloft
    on the mountains
Sea-fogs pitched their tents, and mists from
    the mighty Atlantic   30

Looked on the happy valley, but ne'er from
    their station descended.

There, in the midst of its farms, reposed the
    Acadian village.

Strongly built. were the houses, with frames
    of oak and of hemlock,

Such as the peasants of Normandy° built in
    the reign of the Henries.°

Thatched were the roofs, with dormer-win-
    dows;° and gables projecting   35

Over the basement below protected and shaded
    the doorway.

There in the tranquil evenings of summer,
    when brightly the sunset

Lighted the village street, and gilded the vanes
    on the chimneys,

Matrons and maidens sat in snow-white caps
    and in kirtles°

Scarlet and blue and green, with distaffs° spin-
    ning the golden   40

Flax for the gossiping° looms, whose noisy
    shuttles within doors

Mingled their sound with the whir of the
    wheels and the songs of the maidens.

Solemnly down the street came the parish
    priest, and the children

Paused in their play to kiss the hand he ex-
    tended to bless them.

Reverend walked he among them; and up rose
    matrons and maidens,   45

Hailing his slow approach with words of affectionate welcome.

Then came the laborers home from the field, and serenely the sun sank

Down to his rest, and twilight prevailed. Anon° from the belfry

Softly the Angelus° sounded, and over the roofs of the village

Columns of pale blue smoke, like clouds of incense ascending,   50

Rose from a hundred hearths, the homes of peace and contentment.

Thus dwelt together in love these simple Acadian farmers,—

Dwelt in the love of God and of man. Alike were they free from

Fear, that reigns with the tyrant, and envy, the vice of republics.°

Neither locks had they to their doors, nor bars to their windows;   55

But their dwellings were open as day and the hearts of the owners;

There the richest was poor, and the poorest lived in abundance.

Somewhat apart from the village, and nearer the Basin of Minas,

Benedict Bellefontaine, the wealthiest farmer of Grand-Pré,

Dwelt on his goodly acres; and with him, di-
    recting his household,   60
Gentle Evangeline lived, his child, and the
    pride of the village.
Stalworth° and stately in form was the man of
    seventy winters°;
Hearty and hale was he, an oak that is cov-
    ered with snow-flakes;
White as the snow were his locks, and his
    cheeks as brown as the oak leaves.
Fair was she to behold, that maiden of seven-
    teen summers;   65
Black were her eyes as the berry that grows
    on the thorn by the wayside,
Black, yet how softly they gleamed beneath
    the brown shade of her tresses!
Sweet was her breath as the breath of kine°
    that feed in the meadows.
When in the harvest heat she bore to the reap-
    ers at noontide
Flagons of home-brewed ale, ah! fair in sooth°
    was the maiden.   70
Fairer was she when, on Sunday morn, while
    the bell from its turret
Sprinkled with holy sounds the air, as the
    priest with his hyssop°
Sprinkles the congregation, and scatters bless-
    ings upon them,
Down the long street she passed, with her
    chaplet of beads° and her missal,°

Wearing her Norman cap and her kirtle of
    blue, and the earrings   75
Brought in the olden time from France, and
    since, as an heirloom,
Handed down from mother to child, through
    long generations.
But a celestial brightness—a more ethereal
    beauty—
Shone on her face and encircled her form,
    when, after confession,
Homeward serenely she walked with God's
    benediction upon her.   80
When she had passed, it seemed like the ceas-
    ing of exquisite music.

  Firmly builded with rafters of oak, the house
    of the farmer
Stood on the side of a hill commanding the
    sea; and a shady
Sycamore grew by the door, with a woodbine
    wreathing around it.
Rudely carved was the porch, with seats be-
    neath; and a footpath   85
Led through an orchard wide, and disappeared
    in the meadow.
Under the sycamore-tree were hives overhung
    by a penthouse,°
Such° as the traveller sees in regions remote
    by the roadside,

Built o'er a box for the poor, or the blessed
     image of Mary.
Farther down, on the slope of the hill, was the
     well with its moss-grown   90
Bucket, fastened with iron, and near it a
     trough for the horses.
Shielding the house from storms, on the north,
     were the barns and the farm-yard.
There stood the broad-wheeled wains° and the
     antique° ploughs and the harrows;
There were the folds for the sheep; and there,
     in his feathered seraglio,°
Strutted the lordly turkey, and crowed the cock,
     with the selfsame   95
Voice that in ages of old had startled the peni-
     tent Peter.°
Bursting with hay were the barns, themselves
     a village. In each one
Far o'er the gable projected a roof of thatch;
     and a staircase,
Under the sheltering eaves, led up to the odor-
     ous corn-loft.°
There too the dove-cot stood, with its meek
     and innocent inmates   100
Murmuring ever of love; while above in the
     variant breezes
Numberless noisy weathercocks rattled and
     sang of mutation.°

Thus, at peace with God and the world, the
    farmer of Grand-Pré

Lived on his sunny farm, and Evangeline gov-
    erned his household.

Many a youth, as he knelt in the church and
    opened his missal,   105

Fixed his eyes upon her as the saint of his
    deepest devotion;

Happy was he who might touch her hand or the
    hem of her garment!

Many a suitor came to her door, by the dark-
    ness befriended,°

And, as he knocked and waited to hear the
    sound of her footsteps,

Knew not which beat the louder, his heart or
    the knocker of iron;   110

Or, at the joyous feast of the Patron Saint of
    the village,

Bolder grew, and pressed her hand in the dance
    as he whispered

Hurried words of love, that seemed a part of
    the music.

But among all who came young Gabriel only
    was welcome;

Gabriel Lajeunesse, the son of Basil the black-
    smith,   115

Who was a mighty man in the village, and
    honored of all men;

For since the birth of time,° throughout all
    ages and nations,

Has the craft of the smith been held in repute
     by the people.
Basil was Benedict's friend. Their children
     from earliest childhood
Grew up together as brother and sister; and
     Father Felician,   120
Priest and pedagogue both in the village, had
     taught them their letters
Out of the selfsame book, with the hymns of the
     church and the plain-song.°
But when the hymn was sung, and the daily
     lesson completed,
Swiftly they hurried away to the forge of Basil
     the blacksmith.
There at the door they stood, with wondering
     eyes to behold him   125
Take in his leathern lap the hoof of the horse
     as a plaything,
Nailing the shoe in its place; while near him
     the tire of the cart-wheel
Lay like a fiery snake, coiled round in a circle
     of cinders.
Oft on autumnal eves, when without in the
     gathering darkness
Bursting with light seemed the smithy,°
     through every cranny and crevice,   130
Warm by the forge within they watched the
     laboring bellows,
And as its panting ceased, and the sparks ex-
     pired in the ashes,

Merrily laughed, and said they° were nuns
    going into the chapel.
Oft on sledges in winter, as swift as the swoop
    of the eagle,
Down the hillside bounding, they glided away
    o'er the meadow.   135
Oft in the barns they climbed to the populous
    nests on the rafters,
Seeking with eager eyes that wondrous stone,
    which the swallow
Brings from the shore of the sea to restore the
    sight of its fledglings;
Lucky° was he who found that stone in the
    nest of the swallow!
Thus passed a few swift years, and they no
    longer were children.   140
He was a valiant youth, and his face, like the
    face of the morning,
Gladdened the earth with its light, and ripened
    thought into action.
She was a woman now, with the heart and hopes
    of a woman.
"Sunshine° of Saint Eulalie" was she called;
    for that was the sunshine
Which, as the farmers believed, would load
    their orchards with apples;   145
She, too, would bring to her husband's house
    delight and abundance,
Filling it full of love and the ruddy faces of
    children.

II

Now had the season returned, when the
    nights grow colder and longer,
And the retreating sun the sign of the Scorpion°
    enters.
Birds of passage sailed through the leaden air,
    from the ice-bound,   150
Desolate northern bays to the shores of tropical
    islands.
Harvests were gathered in; and wild with the
    winds of September
Wrestled the trees of the forest, as Jacob° of
    old with the angel.
All the signs foretold a winter long and inclem-
    ent.
Bees, with prophetic instinct of want, had
    hoarded their honey   155
Till the hives overflowed; and the Indian hunt-
    ers asserted
Cold would the winter be, for thick was the
    fur of the foxes.°
Such was the advent of autumn. Then followed
    that beautiful season,
Called by the pious Acadian peasants the Sum-
    mer of All-Saints°!
Filled was the air with a dreamy and magical
    light; and the landscape   160
Lay as if new-created in all the freshness of
    childhood.

Peace seemed to reign upon earth, and the rest-
    less heart of the ocean
Was for a moment consoled. All sounds were
    in harmony blended.
Voices of children at play, the crowing of cocks
    in the farm-yards,
Whir of wings in the drowsy air, and the
    cooing of pigeons, 165
All were subdued and low as the murmurs of
    love, and the great sun
Looked with the eye of love through·the golden
    vapors around him;
While arrayed in its robes of russet and scarlet
    and yellow,
Bright with the sheen of the dew, each glitter-
    ing tree of the forest
Flashed like the plane-tree the Persian°
    adorned with mantles and jewels. 170

  Now recommenced the reign of rest and affec-
    tion and stillness.
Day with its burden and heat had departed, and
    twilight descending
Brought back the evening star to the sky, and
    the herds to the homestead.
Pawing the ground they came, and resting their
    necks on each other,
And with their nostrils distended inhaling the
    freshness of evening. 175

Foremost, bearing the bell, Evangeline's beauti-
    ful heifer,
Proud of her snow-white hide, and the ribbon
    that waved from her collar,
Quietly paced and slow, as if conscious of hu-
    man affection.
Then came the shepherd back with his bleat-
    ing flocks from the seaside,
Where was their favorite pasture. Behind them
    followed the watch-dog,°   180
Patient, full of importance, and grand in the
    pride of his instinct,
Walking from side to side with a lordly air,
    and superbly
Waving his bushy tail, and urging forward the
    stragglers;
Regent° of flocks was he when the shepherd
    slept; their protector,
When from the forest at night, through the
    starry silence the wolves howled.   185
Late, with the rising moon, returned the wains
    from the marshes,
Laden with briny° hay, that filled the air with
    its odor.
Cheerily neighed the steeds, with dew on their
    manes and their fetlocks,°
While aloft on their shoulders the wooden and
    ponderous saddles,
Painted with brilliant dyes, and adorned with
    tassels of crimson,   190

Nodded in bright array, like hollyhocks heavy
  with blossoms.
Patiently stood the cows meanwhile, and
  yielded their udders
Unto the milkmaid's hand; whilst loud and in
  regular cadence
Into the sounding pails the foaming streamlets
  descended.°
Lowing of cattle and peals of laughter were
  heard in the farm-yard,   195
Echoed back by the barns. Anon they sank
  into stillness;
Heavily closed, with a jarring sound, the valves
  of the barn-doors.
Rattled the wooden bars, and all for a season
  was silent.

  In-doors, warm by the wide-mouthed fire-
  place, idly the farmer
Sat in his elbow-chair and watched how the
  flames and the smoke-wreaths   200
Struggled together like foes in a burning city.
  Behind him,
Nodding and mocking along the wall, with ges-
  tures fantastic,
Darted his own huge shadow, and vanished
  away into darkness.
Faces, clumsily carved in oak, on the back of
  his armchair

Laughed in the flickering light; and the pew-
     ter° plates on the dresser°   205
Caught and reflected the flame, as shields of
     armies the sunshine.
Fragments of song the old man sang, and carols
     of Christmas,
Such as at home, in the olden time, his fathers
     before him
Sang in their Norman orchards and bright Bur-
     gundian vineyards.
Close at her father's side was the gentle Evan-
     geline seated,   210
Spinning flax for the loom, that stood in the
     corner behind her.
Silent awhile were its treadles, at rest was its
     diligent shuttle,
While the monotonous drone of the wheel, like
     the drone of a bagpipe,
Followed the old man's song and united the
     fragments together.
As in a church, when the chant of the choir at
     intervals ceases,   215
Footfalls are heard in the aisles, or words of
     the priest at the altar,
So, in each pause of the song, with measured
     motion the clock clicked.

Thus as they sat, there were footsteps heard,
     and, suddenly lifted,

Close at her father's side was the gentle Evangeline seated.

Sounded the wooden latch, and the door swung
    back on its hinges.

Benedict knew by the hob-nailèd shoes it was
    Basil the blacksmith, 220

And by her beating heart Evangeline knew who
    was with him.

"Welcome!" the farmer exclaimed, as their
    footsteps paused on the threshold,

"Welcome, Basil, my friend! Come, take thy
    place on the settle°

Close by the chimney-side, which is always
    empty without thee;

Take from the shelf overhead thy pipe and the
    box of tobacco; 225

Never so much thyself art thou as when through
    the curling

Smoke of the pipe or the forge, thy friendly
    and jovial face gleams

Round and red as the harvest moon through
    the mist of the marshes."

Then, with a smile of content, thus answered
    Basil the blacksmith,

Taking with easy air the accustomed seat by
    the fireside: — 230

"Benedict Bellefontaine, thou hast ever thy
    jest and thy ballad!

Ever in cheerfullest mood art thou, when others
    are filled with

Gloomy forebodings of ill,° and see only ruin
    before them.

Happy art thou, as if every day thou hadst
    picked up a horseshoe."°
Pausing a moment, to take the pipe that Evan-
    geline brought him,   235
And with a coal from the embers had lighted,
    he slowly continued: —
"Four days now are passed since the English
    ships at their anchors
Ride in the Gaspereau's mouth, with their can-
    non pointed against us.
What their design may be is unknown; but all
    are commanded
On the morrow to meet in the church, where
    his Majesty's mandate°   240
Will be proclaimed as law in the land. Alas!
    in the mean time
Many surmises of evil alarm the hearts of the
    people."
Then made answer the farmer: — "Perhaps
    some friendlier purpose
Brings these ships to our shores. Perhaps the
    harvests in England
By untimely rains or untimelier heat have been
    blighted,   245
And from our bursting barns they would feed .
    their cattle and children."
"Not so thinketh the folk in the village," said,
    warmly, the blacksmith,
Shaking his head, as in doubt; then, heaving a
    sigh, he continued: —

"Louisburg° is not forgotten, nor Beau Séjour,ª
    nor Port Royal.°
Many already have fled to the forest, and lurk
    on its outskirts,   250
Waiting with anxious hearts the dubious fate
    of to-morrow.
Arms have been taken from us, and warlike
    weapons of all kinds;
Nothing is left but the blacksmith's sledge and
    the scythe of the mower."
Then with a pleasant smile made answer the
    jovial farmer: —
"Safer are we unarmed, in the midst of our
    flocks and our cornfields,   255
Safer within these peaceful dikes, besieged by
    the ocean,
Than our fathers in forts, besieged by the
    enemy's cannon.
Fear no evil, my friend, and to-night may no
    shadow of sorrow
Fall on this house and hearth; for this is the
    night of the contract.°
Built are the house and the barn. The merry
    lads of the village   260
Strongly have built them and well; and, break-
    ing the glebe° round about them,
Filled the barn with hay, and the house with
    food for a twelvemonth.
René Leblanc will be here anon, with his papers
    and inkhorn.°

Shall we not then be glad, and rejoice in the
    joy of our children?"
As apart by the window she stood, with her
    hand in her lover's,   265
Blushing Evangeline heard the words that her
    father had spoken,
And, as they died on his lips, the worthy no-
    tary° entered.

III

  Bent like a laboring oar, that toils in the
    surf of the ocean,
Bent, but not broken, by age was the form of
    the notary public;
Shocks of yellow hair, like the silken floss of
    the maize, hung   270
Over his shoulders; his forehead was high; and
    glasses with horn bows
Sat astride on his nose, with a look of wisdom
    supernal.°
Father of twenty children was he, and more
    than a hundred
Children's children rode on his knee, and heard
    his great watch tick.
Four long years in the times of the war had
    he languished a captive,   275
Suffering much in an old French fort as the
    friend of the English.

Now, though warier grown, without all guile
    or suspicion,
Ripe in wisdom was he, but patient, and simple,
    and childlike.
He was beloved by all, and most of all by the
    children;
For he told them tales of the Loup-garou° in
    the forest,   280
And of the goblin that came in the night to
    water the horses,
And of the white Létiche, the ghost of a child
    who unchristened
Died, and was doomed to haunt unseen the
    chambers of children;
And how on Christmas evé the oxen talked in
    the stable,
And how the fever was cured by a spider shut
    up in a nutshell,   285
And of the marvellous powers of four-leaved
    clover and horseshoes,
With whatsoever else was writ in the lore° of
    the village.
Then up rose from his seat by the fireside
    Basil the blacksmith,
Knocked from his pipe the ashes, and slowly
    extending his right hand,
"Father Leblanc," he exclaimed, "thou hast
    heard the talk in the village,   290
And, perchance, canst tell us some news of
    these ships and their errand."

Then with modest demeanor made answer the
    notary public, —

"Gossip enough have I heard, in sooth, yet am
    never the wiser;

And what their errand may be I know not
    better than others.

Yet am I not of those who imagine some evil
    intention   295

Brings them here, for we are at peace, and
    why then molest us?"

"God's name!" shouted the hasty and some-
    what irascible° blacksmith;

"Must we in all things look for the how, and
    the why, and the wherefore?

Daily injustice is done, and might is the right
    of the strongest!"

But without heeding his warmth, continued
    the notary public,—   300

"Man is unjust, but God is just; and finally
    justice

Triumphs; and well I remember a story, that
    often consoled me,

When as a captive I lay in the old French fort
    at Port Royal."

This was the old man's favorite tale, and he
    loved to repeat it

When his neighbors complained that any in-
    justice was done them.   305

"Once in an ancient city,° whose name I no
    longer remember,

Raised aloft on a column, a brazen statue of
    Justice
Stood in the public square, upholding the scales
    in its left hand,
And in its right a sword, as an emblem that
    justice presided
Over the laws of the land, and the hearts and
    homes of the people.   310
Even the birds had built their nests in the
    scales of the balance,
Having no fear of the sword that flashed in
    the sunshine above them.
But in the course of time the laws of the land
    were corrupted;
Might took the place of right, and the weak
    were oppressed, and the mighty
Ruled with an iron rod. Then it chanced in a
    nobleman's palace   315
That a necklace of pearls was lost, and ere
    long a suspicion
Fell on an orphan girl who lived as a maid in
    the household.
She, after form of trial condemned to die on
    the scaffold,
Patiently met her doom at the foot of the
    statue of Justice.
As to her Father in heaven her innocent spirit
    ascended,   320
Lo! o'er the city a tempest rose; and the bolts
    of the thunder

Smote the statue of bronze, and hurled in wrath from its left hand

Down on the pavement below the clattering scales of the balance,

And in the hollow thereof was found the nest of a magpie,

Into whose clay-built walls the necklace of pearls was inwoven." 325

Silenced, but not convinced, when the story was ended, the blacksmith

Stood like a man who fain would speak, but findeth no language;

All his thoughts were congealed into lines on his face, as the vapors

Freeze in fantastic shapes on the window-panes in the winter.

Then Evangeline lighted the brazen lamp on the table, 330

Filled, till it overflowed, the pewter tankard with home-brewed

Nut-brown ale, that was famed for its strength in the village of Grand-Pré;

While from his pocket the notary drew his papers and inkhorn,

Wrote with a steady hand the date and the age of the parties,°

Naming the dower° of the bride in flocks of sheep and in cattle.

Orderly all things proceeded, and duly and
    well were completed,
And the great seal of the law was set like a
    sun on the margin.
Then from his leathern pouch the farmer threw
    on the table
Three times the old man's fee in solid pieces
    of silver;
And the notary rising, and blessing the bride
    and bridegroom,   340
Lifted aloft the tankard of ale and drank to
    their welfare.
Wiping the foam from his lip, he solemnly
    bowed and departed,
While in silence the others sat and mused by
    the fireside,
Till Evangeline brought the draught-board°
    out of its corner.
Soon the game begun. In friendly contention
    the old men   345
Laughed at each lucky hit, or successful ma-
    nœuvre,°
Laughed when a man was crowned, or a breach
    was made in the king-row.
Meanwhile apart, in the twilight gloom of a
    window's embrasure,°
Sat the lovers and whispered together, behold-
    ing the moon rise
Over the pallid sea and the silvery mist of the
    meadows.   350

Silently one by one, in the infinite meadows
    of heaven,
Blossomed the lovely stars, the forget-me-nots
    of the angels.

    Thus was the evening passed. Anon the bell
    from the belfry
Rang out the hour of nine, the village curfew,°
    and straightway
Rose the guests and departed; and silence
    reigned in the household.   355
Many a farewell word and sweet good-night
    on the door-step
Lingered long in Evangeline's heart, and filled
    it with gladness.
Carefully then were covered the embers that
    glowed on the hearth-stone,
And on the oaken stairs resounded the tread
    of the farmer.
Soon with a soundless step the foot of Evan-
    geline followed.   360
Up the staircase moved a luminous space in
    the darkness,
Lighted less by the lamp than the shining face
    of the maiden.
Silent she passed through the hall, and entered
    the door of her chamber.
Simple that chamber was, with its curtains of
    white, and its clothes-press

Ample and high, on whose spacious shelves
    were carefully folded   ₃₆₅
Linen and woollen stuffs, by the hand of Evan-
    geline woven.
This was the precious dower she would bring
    to her husband in marriage,
Better than flocks and herds, being proofs of
    her skill as a housewife.
Soon she extinguished her lamp, for the mel-
    low and radiant moonlight
Streamed through the windows, and lighted
    the room, till the heart of the maiden   ₃₇₀
Swelled and obeyed its power, like the tremu-
    lous tides of the ocean.
Ah! she was fair, exceeding fair to behold, as
    she stood with
Naked snow-white feet on the gleaming floor
    of her chamber!
Little she dreamed that below, among the
    trees of the orchard,
Waited her lover and watched for the gleam
    of her lamp and her shadow.   ₃₇₅
Yet were her thoughts of him, and at times a
    feeling of sadness°
Passed o'er her soul, as the sailing shade of
    clouds in the moonlight
Flitted across the floor and darkened the room
    for a moment.
And, as she gazed from the window, she saw
    serenely the moon pass

Forth from the folds of a cloud, and one star
    follow her footsteps,   380
As out of Abraham's tent young Ishmael wan-
    dered with Hagar°!

IV

  Pleasantly rose next morning the sun on the
    village of Grand-Pré.
Pleasantly gleamed in the soft, sweet air the
    Basin of Minas.
Where the ships, with their wavering shadows,
    were riding at anchor.
Life had long been astir in the village, and
    clamorous labor   385
Knocked with its hundred hands° at the golden
    gates of the morning.
Now from the country around, from the farms
    and neighboring hamlets,
Came in their holiday dresses the blithe
    Acadian peasants.
Many a glad good-morrow and jocund° laugh
    from the young folk
Made the bright air brighter, as up from the
    numerous meadows,   390
Where no path could be seen but the track of
    wheels in the greensward,
Group after group appeared, and joined, or
    passed on the highway.

Long ere noon, in the village all sounds of
    labor were silenced.
Thronged were the streets with people; and
    noisy groups at the house-doors
Sat in the cheerful sun, and rejoiced and gos-
    siped together.   395
Every house was an inn, where all were wel-
    comed and feasted;
For with this simple people, who lived like
    brothers together,
All things were held in common, and what one
    had was another's.
Yet under Benedict's roof hospitality seemed
    more abundant:
For Evangeline stood among the guests of her
    father;   400
Bright was her face with smiles and words of
    welcome and gladness
Fell from her beautiful lips, and blessed the
    cup as she gave it.

Under the open sky, in the odorous air of
    the orchard,
Stript of its golden fruit, was spread the feast
    of betrothal.
There in the shade of the porch were the priest
    and the notary seated;   405
There good Benedict sat, and sturdy Basil the
    blacksmith.

Not far withdrawn from these, by the cider-
    press and the beehives,
Michael the fiddler was placed, with the gayest
    of hearts and of waistcoats.
Shadow and light from the leaves alternately
    played on his snow-white
Hair, as it waved in the wind; and the jolly
    face of the fiddler   410
Glowed like a living coal when the ashes are
    blown from the embers.
Gayly the old man sang to the vibrant sound
    of his fiddle.
Tous les Bourgeois de Chartres,° and *Le Caril-*
    lon de Dunquerque,°
And anon with his wooden shoes beat time to
    the music.
Merrily, merrily whirled the wheels of the
    dizzying dances   415
Under the orchard-trees and down the path to
    the meadows;
Old folk and young together, and children
    mingled among them.
Fairest of all the maids was Evangeline, Bene-
    dict's daughter!
Noblest of all the youths was Gabriel, son of
    the blacksmith!

So passed the morning away. And lo! with
    a summons sonorous   420

Not far withdrawn from these, by the ciderpress and the
    beehives,
Michael the fiddler was placed . . .

Sounded the bell from its tower, and over the
    meadows a drum beat.

Thronged ere long was the church with men.
    Without, in the churchyard,

Waited the women. They stood by the graves,
    and hung on the headstones

Garlands of autumn-leaves and evergreens
    fresh from the forest.

Then came the guard from the ships, and
    marching proudly among them   425

Entered the sacred portal. With loud and dis-
    sonant clangor

Echoed the sound of their brazen drums from
    ceiling and casement, —

Echoed a moment only, and slowly the pon-
    derous portal

Closed, and in silence the crowd awaited the
    will of the soldiers.

Then uprose their commander,° and spake
    from the steps of the altar,   430

Holding aloft in his hands, with its seal, the
    royal commission.

"You are convened this day," he said, "by
    his Majesty's orders.

Clement and kind has he been; but how you
    have answered his kindness,

Let your own hearts reply! To my natural
    make and my temper

Painful the task is I do, which to you I know
    must be grievous.   435

Yet must I bow and obey, and deliver the will
    of our monarch:
Namely, that all your lands, and dwellings,
    and cattle of all kinds
Forfeited be to the crown; and that you your-
    selves from this province
Be transported to other lands. God grant you
    may dwell there
Ever as faithful subjects, a happy and peace-
    able people!   440
Prisoners now I declare you; for such is his
    Majesty's pleasure!"
As, when the air is serene in the sultry solstice°
    of summer,
Suddenly gathers a storm, and the deadly sling
    of the hailstones
Beats down the farmer's corn in the field and
    shatters his windows.
Hiding the sun, and strewing the ground with
    thatch from the house-roofs,   445
Bellowing fly the herds, and seek to break
    their enclosures;
So on the hearts of the people descended the
    words of the speaker.
Silent a moment they stood in speechless won-
    der, and then rose
Louder and ever louder a wail of sorrow and
    anger,
And, by one impulse moved, they madly rushed
    to the door-way.   450

Vain was the hope of escape; and cries and
    fierce imprecations°
Rang through the house of prayer; and high
    o'er the heads of the others
Rose, with his arms uplifted, the figure of
    Basil the blacksmith,
As, on a stormy sea, a spar is tossed by the
    billows.
Flushed was his face and distorted with pas-
    sion; and wildly he shouted, —   455
"Down with the tyrants of England! we never
    have sworn them allegiance!
Death to these foreign soldiers, who seize on
    our homes and our harvests!"
More he fain would have said, but the merci-
    less hand of a soldier
Smote him upon the mouth, and dragged him
    down to the pavement.

In the midst of the strife and tumult of
    angry contention,   460
Lo! the door of the chancel° opened, and
    Father Felician
Entered, with serious mien,° and ascended the
    steps of the altar.
Raising his reverend hand, with a gesture he
    awed into silence
All that clamorous throng; and thus he spake
    to his people;

Deep were his tones and solemn; in accents
    measured and mournful   ₄₆₅
Spake he, as, after the tocsin's° alarum,° dis-
    tinctly the clock strikes.
"What is this that ye do, my children? what
    madness has seized you?
Forty years of my life have I labored among
    you, and taught you,
Not in word alone, but in deed, to love one
    another!
Is this the fruit of my toils, of my vigils and
    prayers and privations?   ₄₇₀
Have you so soon forgotten all lessons of love
    and forgiveness?
This is the house of the Prince of Peace, and
    would you profane it
Thus with violent deeds and hearts overflow-
    ing with hatred?
Lo! where the crucified Christ from His cross
    is gazing upon you!
See! in those sorrowful eyes what meekness
    and holy compassion!   ₄₇₅
Hark! how those lips still repeat the prayer,
    'O Father, forgive them!'
Let us repeat that prayer in the hour when the
    wicked assail us,
Let us repeat it now, and say, 'O Father, for-
    give them!'"
Few were his words of rebuke, but deep in
    the hearts of his people

Sank they, and sobs of contrition° succeeded
the passionate outbreak, 480
While they repeated his prayer, and said, "O
Father, forgive them!"

Then came the evening service. The tapers
gleamed from the altar.
Fervent and deep was the voice of the priest,
and the people responded,
Not with their lips alone, but their hearts; and
the Ave Maria°
Sang they, and fell on their knees, and their
souls, with devotion translated,° 485
Rose on the ardor of prayer, like Elijah as-
cending to heaven.

Meanwhile had spread in the village the tid-
ings of ill, and on all sides
Wandered, wailing, from house to house the
women and children.
Long at her father's door Evangeline stood,
with her right hand
Shielding her eyes from the level rays of the
sun, that, descending, 490
Lighted the village street with mysterious
splendor, and roofed each
Peasant's cottage with golden thatch, and em-
blazoned° its windows.
Long within had been spread the snow-white
cloth on the table;

There stood the wheaten loaf, and the honey
    fragrant with wild-flowers;

There stood the tankard of ale, and the cheese
    fresh brought from the dairy,   495

And, at the head of the board, the great arm-
    chair of the farmer.

Thus did Evangeline wait at her father's door,
    as the sunset

Threw the long shadows of trees o'er the broad
    ambrosial° meadows.

Ah! on her spirit within a deeper shadow had
    fallen,

And from the fields of her soul a fragrance
    celestial ascended, —   500

Charity, meekness, love, and hope, and for-
    giveness, and patience!

Then, all-forgetful of self, she wandered into
    the village,

Cheering with looks and words the mournful
    hearts of the women,

As o'er the darkening fields with lingering steps
    they departed,

Urged by their household cares, and the weary
    feet of their children.   505

Down sank the great red sun, and in golden,
    glimmering vapors

Veiled the light of his face, like the Prophet°
    descending from Sinai.

Sweetly over the village the bell of the An-
    gelus sounded.

Meanwhile, amid the gloom, by the church
　　Evangeline lingered.
All was silent within; and in vain at the door
　　and the windows　　510
Stood she, and listened and looked, till, over-
　　come by emotion,
"Gabriel!" cried she aloud with tremulous
　　voice; but no answer
Came from the graves of the dead, nor the
　　gloomier grave° of the living.
Slowly at length she returned to the tenantless
　　house of her father.
Smoldered the fire on the hearth, on the board
　　was the supper untasted.　　515
Empty and drear was each room, and haunted
　　with phantoms of terror.
Sadly echoed her step on the stair and the
　　floor of her chamber.°
In the dead of the night she heard the discon-
　　solate rain fall
Loud on the withered leaves of the sycamore-
　　tree by the window.
Keenly the lightning flashed; and the voice of
　　the echoing thunder　　520
Told her that God was in heaven, and gov-
　　erned the world He created!
Then she remembered the tale she had heard
　　of the justice of Heaven;
Soothed was her troubled soul, and she peace-
　　fully slumbered till morning.

V

Four times the sun had risen and set; and
    now on the fifth day
Cheerily called the cock to the sleeping maids
    of the farm-house.   525
Soon o'er the yellow fields, in silent and mourn-
    ful procession,
Came from the neighboring hamlets and farms
    the Acadian women,
Driving in ponderous wains their household
    goods to the sea-shore,
Pausing and looking back to gaze once more
    on their dwellings,
Ere they were shut from sight by the winding
    road and the woodland.   530
Close at their sides their children ran, and
    urged on the oxen,
While in their little hands they clasped some
    fragments of playthings.

Thus to the Gaspereau's mouth they hur-
    ried; and there on the sea-beach
Piled in confusion lay the household goods of
    the peasants.
All day long between the shore and the ships
    did the boats ply;   535
All day long the wains came laboring down
    from the village.

Late in the afternoon, when the sun was near
    to his setting,
Echoed far o'er the fields came the roll of
    drums from the churchyard.
Thither the women and children thronged. On
    a sudden the church-doors
Opened, and forth came the guard, and march-
    ing in gloomy procession   540
Followed the long-imprisoned, but patient,
    Acadian farmers.
Even as pilgrims, who journey afar from their
    homes and their country,
Sing as they go, and in singing forget they are
    weary and wayworn,
So with songs on their lips the Acadian peas-
    ants descended
Down from the church to the shore, amid their
    wives and their daughters.   545
Foremost the young men came; and, raising
    together their voices,
Sang with tremulous lips a chant of the Cath-
    olic Missions: —
"Sacred heart of the Saviour! O inexhaustible
    fountain!
Fill our hearts this day with strength and sub-
    mission and patience!"
Then the old men, as they marched, and the
    women that stood by the wayside   550
Joined in the sacred psalm, and the birds in
    the sunshine above them

Mingled their notes therewith, like voices of
　　spirits departed.

　Half-way down to the shore Evangeline
　　waited in silence,
Not overcome with grief, but strong in the
　　hour of affliction, —
Calmly and sadly she waited, until the pro-
　　cession approached her,　　　555
And she beheld the face of Gabriel pale with
　　emotion.
Tears then filled her eyes, and, eagerly run-
　　ning to meet him,
Clasped she his hands, and laid her head on
　　his shoulder, and whispered, —
"Gabriel! be of good cheer! for if we love one
　　another
Nothing, in truth, can harm us, whatever mis-
　　chances may happen!"　　　560
Smiling she spake° these words; then suddenly
　　paused, for her father
Saw she slowly advancing. Alas! how changed
　　was his aspect!
Gone was the glow from his cheek, and the
　　fire from his eye, and his footstep
Heavier seemed with the weight of the heavy
　　heart in his bosom.
But with a smile and a sigh, she clasped his
　　neck and embraced him,　　　565

While in despair on the shore Evangeline stood with
her father.

Speaking words of endearment where words
of comfort availed not.
Thus to the Gaspereau's mouth moved on that
mournful procession.

There disorder prevailed, and the tumult
and stir of embarking.
Busily plied the freighted boats; and in the
confusion
Wives were torn from their husbands, and
mothers, too late, saw their children 570
Left on the land, extending their arms, with
wildest entreaties.
So unto separate ships were Basil and Gabriel
carried.
While in despair on the shore Evangeline stood
with her father.
Half the task was not done when the sun went
down, and the twilight
Deepened and darkened around; and in haste
the refluent° ocean 575
Fled away from the shore, and left the line of
the sand-beach
Covered with waifs° of the tide, with kelp°
and the slippery sea-weed.
Farther back in the midst of the household
goods and the wagons,
Like to a gypsy camp, or a leaguer° after a
battle,

All escape cut off by the sea, and the sentinels
    near them,   580
Lay encamped for the night the houseless
    Acadian farmers.
Back to its nethermost caves retreated the
    bellowing ocean,
Dragging adown the beach the rattling pebbles,
    and leaving
Inland and far up the shore the stranded boats
    of the sailors.
Then, as the night descended, the herds re-
    turned from their pastures;   585
Sweet was the moist still air with the odor of
    milk from their udders;
Lowing they waited, and long, at the well-
    known bars of the farm-yard, —
Waited and looked in vain for the voice and
    the hand of the milkmaid.
Silence reigned in the streets; from the church
    no Angelus sounded,
Rose no smoke from the roofs, and gleamed
    no lights from the windows.   590

But on the shores meanwhile the evening fires
    had been kindled,
Built of the drift-wood thrown on the sands
    from wrecks in the tempest.
Round them shapes of gloom and sorrowful
    faces were gathered,

Voices of women were heard, and of men, and
the crying of children.

Onward from fire to fire, as from hearth to
hearth in his parish, 595

Wandered the faithful priest, consoling and
blessing and cheering,

Like unto shipwrecked Paul on Melita's deso-
late seashore.°

Thus he approached the place where Evangeline
sat with her father,

And in the flickering light beheld the face of
the old man,

Haggard and hollow and wan, and without
either thought or emotion, 600

E'en as the face of a clock from which the
hands have been taken.°

Vainly Evangeline strove with words and ca-
resses to cheer him,

Vainly offered him food; yet he moved not, he
looked not, he spake not,

But, with a vacant stare, ever gazed at the
flickering fire-light.

"Benedicite!"° murmured the priest, in tones
of compassion. 605

More he fain would have said, but his heart
was full, and his accents

Faltered and paused on his lips, as the feet of
a child on a threshold,

Hushed by the scene he beholds, and the awful
presence of sorrow.

Silently, therefore, he laid his hand on the head
    of the maiden,
Raising his eyes, full of tears, to the silent stars
    that above them   610
Moved on their way, unperturbed by the
    wrongs and sorrows of mortals.
Then sat he down at her side, and they wept
    together in silence.   ʹ

  Suddenly rose from the south a light, as in
    autumn the blood-red
Moon climbs the crystal walls of heaven, and
    o'er the horizon
Titan-like° stretches its hundred hands upon
    mountain and meadow,   615
Seizing the rocks and the rivers, and piling
    huge shadows together.
Broader and ever broader it gleamed on the
    roofs of the village,
Gleamed on the sky and the sea, and the ships
    that lay in the roadstead.°
Columns of shining smoke uprose, and flashes
    of flame were
Thrust through their folds and withdrawn, like
    the quivering hands of a martyr.   620
Then as the wind seized the gleeds° and the
    burning thatch, and, uplifting,
Whirled them aloft through the air, at once
    from a hundred house-tops

Started the sheeted smoke with flashes of flame
    intermingled.

  These things beheld in dismay the crowd on
    the shore and on shipboard.
Speechless at first they stood, then cried aloud
    in their anguish,   625
"We shall behold no more our homes in the
    village of Grand-Pré!"
Loud on a sudden the cocks began to crow in
    the farm-yards,
Thinking the day had dawned; and anon the
    lowing of cattle
Came on the evening breeze, by the barking
    of dogs interrupted.
Then rose a sound of dread, such as startles
    the sleeping encampments   630
Far in the western prairies or forests that skirt
    the Nebraska,
When the wild horses affrighted sweep by with
    the speed of the whirlwind,
Or the loud bellowing herds of buffaloes rush
    to the river.
Such was the sound that arose on the night,
    as the herds and the horses
Broke through their folds and fences, and
    madly rushed o'er the meadows.   635

  Overwhelmed with the sight, yet speechless,
    the priest and the maiden

Gazed on the scene of terror that reddened and
   widened before them;
And as they turned at length to speak to their
   silent companion,
Lo! from his seat he had fallen, and stretched
   abroad on the sea-shore
Motionless lay his form, from which the soul
   had departed.   640
Slowly the priest uplifted the lifeless head, and
   the maiden
Knelt at her father's side, and wailed aloud in
   her terror.
Then in a swoon she sank, and lay with her
   head on his bosom.
Through the long night she lay in deep, ob-
   livious° slumber;
And when she woke from the trance, she be-
   held a multitude near her.   645
Faces of friends she beheld, that were mourn-
   fully gazing upon her,
Pallid, with tearful eyes, and looks of saddest
   compassion.
Still the blaze of the burning village illumined
   the landscape,
Reddened the sky overhead, and gleamed on
   the faces around her,
And like the day of doom it seemed to her
   wavering senses.   650
Then a familiar voice she heard, as it said to
   the people, —

"Let us bury him here by the sea. When a happier season

Brings us again to our homes from the unknown land of our exile,

Then shall his sacred dust be piously laid in the churchyard."

Such were the words of the priest. And there in haste by the sea-side,   655

Having the glare of the burning village for funeral torches,

But without bell or book, they buried the farmer of Grand Pré.

And as the voice of the priest repeated the service of sorrow,

Lo! with a mournful sound, like the voice of a vast congregation,

Solemnly answered the sea, and mingled its roar with the dirges°   660

'Twas the returning tide, that afar from the waste of the ocean,

With the first dawn of the day, came heaving and hurrying landward.

Then recommenced once more the stir and noise of embarking;

And with the ebb of the tide the ships sailed out of the harbor,

Leaving behind them the dead on the shore, and the village in ruins.   665

PART THE SECOND

I

Many a weary year had passed since the burn-
    ing of Grand-Pré,
When on the falling tide the freighted vessels
    departed,
Bearing a nation, with all its household gods,°
    into exile,
Exile without an end, and without an example
    in story.
Far asunder, on separate coasts, the Acadians
    landed;   670
Scattered were they, like flakes of snow, when
    the wind from the northeast
Strikes aslant through the fogs that darken
    the Banks of Newfoundland.
Friendless, homeless, hopeless, they wandered
    from city to city,
From the cold lakes of the North to sultry
    Southern savannas,°—
From the bleak shores of the sea to the lands
    where the Father of Waters°   675
Seizes the hills in his hands, and drags them
    down to the ocean,

Deep in their sands to bury the scattered bones
    of the mammoth.°

Friends they sought and homes; and many,
    despairing, heart-broken,

Asked of the earth but a grave, and no longer
    a friend nor a fireside.

Written their history stands on tablets of stone
    in the churchyards.   680

Long among them was seen a maiden who
    waited and wandered,

Lowly and meek in spirit, and patiently suf-
    fering all things.

Fair was she and young; but, alas! before her
    extended,

Dreary and vast and silent, the desert of life,
    with its pathway

Marked by the graves of those who had sor-
    rowed and suffered before her,   685

Passions long extinguished, and hopes long
    dead and abandoned,

As the emigrant's way o'er the Western desert
    is marked by

Camp-fires long consumed, and bones that
    bleach in the sunshine.

Something there was in her life incomplete,
    imperfect, unfinished;

As if a morning of June, with all its music and
    sunshine,   690

Suddenly paused in the sky, and, fading, slowly
    descended

Into the east again, from whence it late had
    arisen.
Sometimes she lingered in towns, till, urged by
    the fever within her,
Urged by a restless longing, the hunger and
    thirst of the spirit,
She would commence again her endless search
    and endeavor;   695
Sometimes in churchyards strayed, and gazed
    on the crosses and tombstònes,
Sat by some nameless grave, and thought that
    perhaps in its bosom
He was already at rest, and she longed to slum-
    ber beside him.
Sometimes a rumor, a hearsay, an inarticulate
    whisper,
Came with its airy hand to point and beckon
    her forward.   700
Sometimes she spake with those who had seen
    her beloved and known him,
But it was long ago, in some far-off place or
    forgotten.
"Gabriel Lajeunesse!" they said; "Oh, yes! we
    have seen him.
He was with Basil the blacksmith, and both
    have gone to the prairies;
Coureurs-des-bois° are they, and famous hunt-
    ers and trappers."   705
"Gabriel Lajeunesse!" said others; "Oh, yes!
    we have seen him.

He is a voyageur° in the lowlands of Louisi-
    ana."
Then would they say, "Dear child! why dream
    and wait for him longer?
Are there not other youths as fair as Gabriel?
    others
Who have hearts as tender and true, and spirits
    as loyal? 710
Here is Baptiste Leblanc, the notary's son, who
    has loved thee
Many a tedious year; come, give him thy hand
    and be happy!
Thou art too fair to be left to braid St. Cath-
    erine's tresses."°
Then would Evangeline answer, serenely but
    sadly, "I cannot!
Whither my heart has gone, there follows my
    hand, and not elsewhere. 715
For when the heart goes before, like a lamp,
    and illumines the pathway,
Many things are made clear, that else lie hid-
    den in darkness."
Thereupon the priest, her friend and father
    confessor,
Said, with a smile, "O daughter! thy God thus
    speaketh within thee!
Talk not of wasted affection, affection never
    was wasted; 720
If it enrich not the heart of another, its waters,
    returning

Back to their springs, like the rain, shall fill
    them full of refreshment;
That which the fountain sends forth returns
    again to the fountain.
Patience; accomplish thy labor; accomplish
    thy work of affection!
Sorrow and silence are strong, and patient en-
    durance is godlike.   725
Therefore accomplish thy labor of love, till the
    heart is made godlike,
Purified, strengthened, perfected, and rendered
    more worthy of heaven!"
Cheered by the good man's words, Evangeline
    labored and waited.
Still in her heart she heard the funeral dirge
    of the ocean,
But with its sound there was mingled a voice
    that whispered, "Despair not!"   730
Thus did that poor soul wander in want and
    cheerless discomfort,
Bleeding, barefooted, over the shards° and
    thorns of existence.
Let me essay,° O Muse! to follow the wan-
    derer's footsteps; —
Not through each devious° path, each change-
    ful year of existence;
But as a traveller follows a streamlet's course
    through the valley: 735
Far from its margin at times, and seeing the
    gleam of its water

Here and there, in some open space, and at
 intervals only;
Then drawing nearer its banks, through sylvan
 glooms that conceal it,
Though he behold it not, he can hear its con-
 tinuous murmur;
Happy, at length, if he find the spot where it
 reaches an outlet.   740

II

It was the month of May. Far down the
 Beautiful River,°
Past the Ohio shore and past the mouth of the
 Wabash,
Into the golden stream of the broad and swift
 Mississippi,
Floated a cumbrous boat, that was rowed by
 Acadian boatmen.
It was a band of exiles: a raft as it were, from
 the shipwrecked   745
Nation, scattered along the coast, now floating
 together,
Bound by the bonds of a common belief and
 a common misfortune;
Men and women and children, who, guided by
 hope or by hearsay,
Sought for their kith and their kin° among the
 few-acred farmers

On the Acadian coast, and the prairies of fair
    Opelousas.°   750
With them Evangeline went, and her guide, the
    Father Felician.
Onward o'er sunken sands, through a wilder-
    ness sombre with forests,
Day after day they glided adown the turbu-
    lent river;
Night after night, by their blazing fires, en-
    camped on its borders.
Now through rushing chutes, among green
    islands, where plumelike   755
Cotton-trees nodded their shadowy crests, they
    swept with the current,
Then emerged into broad lagoons, where sil-
    very sand-bars
Lay in the stream, and along the wimpling°
    waves of their margin,
Shining with snow-white plumes, large flocks
    of pelicans waded.
Level the landscape grew, and along the shores
    of the river,   760
Shaded by china-trees,° in the midst of lux-
    uriant gardens,
Stood the houses of planters, with negro-cabins
    and dove-cots.
They were approaching the region where reigns
    perpetual summer,
Where through the Golden Coast, and groves
    of orange and citron,

Sweeps with majestic curve the river away to
    the eastward. 765

They, too, swerved from their course; and en-
    tering the Bayou of Plaquemine,

Soon were lost in a maze of sluggish and devious
    waters,

Which, like a network of steel, extended in
    every direction.

Over their heads the towering and tenebrous°
    boughs of the cypress

Met in a dusky arch, and trailing mosses in
    mid-air 770

Waved like banners that hang on the walls of
    ancient cathedrals.

Deathlike the silence seemed, and unbroken,
    save by the herons

Home to their roosts in the cedar-trees return-
    ing at sunset,

Or by the owl, as he greeted the moon with
    demoniac° laughter.

Lovely the moonlight was as it glanced and
    gleamed on the water, 775

Gleamed on the columns of cypress and cedar
    sustaining the arches,

Down through whose broken vaults it fell as
    through chinks in a ruin.

Dreamlike, and indistinct, and strange were all
    things around them;

And o'er their spirits there came a feeling of
    wonder and sadness, —

Strange forebodings of ill, unseen and that
    cannot be compassed. ₇₈₀
As, at the tramp of a horse's hoof on the turf
    of the prairies,
Far in advance are closed the leaves of the
    shrinking mimosa,°
So, at the hoof-beats of fate, with sad forebod-
    ings of evil,
Shrinks and closes the heart, ere the stroke of
    doom has attained it.
But Evangeline's heart was sustained by a vi-
    sion, that faintly ₇₈₅
Floated before her eyes, and beckoned her on
    through the moonlight.
It was the thought of her brain that assumed
    the shape of a phantom.
Through those shadowy aisles had Gabriel
    wandered before her,
And every stroke of the oar now brought him
    nearer and nearer.

Then in his place, at the prow of the boat,
    rose one of the oarsmen, ₇₉₀
And, as a signal sound, if others like them per-
    adventure°
Sailed on those gloomy and midnight streams,
    blew a blast on his bugle.
Wild through the dark colonnades° and corri-
    dors leafy the blast rang,

Breaking the seal of silence and giving tongues
    to the forest.
Soundless above them the banners of moss just
    stirred to the music.   795
Multitudinous echoes awoke and died in the
    distance,
Over the watery floor, and beneath the rever-
    berant° branches;
But not a voice replied; no answer came from
    the darkness;
And, when the echoes had ceased, like a sense
    of pain was the silence.
Then Evangeline slept; but the boatmen rowed
    through the midnight,   800
Silent at times, then singing familiar Canadian
    boat-songs,
Such as they sang of old on their own Acadian
    rivers,
While through the night were heard the mys-
    terious sounds of the desert,
Far off, — indistinct, — as of wave or wind
    in the forest,
Mixed with the whoop of the crane and the
    roar of the grim alligator.   805

    Thus ere another noon they emerged from
    the shades; and before them
Lay, in the golden sun, the lakes of the Atcha-
    falaya.

Water-lilies in myriads rocked on the slight un-
    dulations
Made by the passing oars, and, resplendent in
    beauty, the lotus
Lifted her golden crown above the heads of
    the boatmen.   810
Faint was the air with the odorous breath of
    magnolia blossoms,
And with the heat of noon; and numberless
    sylvan islands,
Fragrant and thickly embowered with blossom-
    ing hedges of roses,
Near to whose shores they glided along, in-
    vited to slumber.°
Soon by the fairest of these their weary oars
    were suspended.   815
Under the boughs of Wachita willows, that
    grew by the margin,
Safely their boat was moored; and scattered
    about on the greensward,
Tired with their midnight toil, the weary trav-
    ellers slumbered.
Over them vast and high extended the cope°
    of a cedar.
Swinging from its great arms, the trumpet-
    flower and the grapevine   820
Hung their ladder of ropes aloft like the ladder
    of Jacob,
On whose pendulous° stairs the angels ascend-
    ing, descending,

Were the swift humming-birds, that flitted
    from blossom to blossom.
Such was the vision Evangeline saw as she
    slumbered beneath it.
Filled was her heart with love, and the dawn
    of an opening heaven   ₈₂₅
Lighted her soul in sleep with the glory of re-
    gions celestial.

Nearer, and ever nearer, among the number-
    less islands,
Darted a light, swift boat, that sped away o'er
    the water,
Urged on its course by the sinewy arms of
    hunters and trappers.
Northward its prow was turned, to the land
    of the bison and beaver.   ₈₃₀
At the helm sat a youth, with countenance
    thoughtful and careworn.
Dark and neglected locks overshadowed his
    brow, and a sadness
Somewhat beyond his years on his face was
    legibly written.
Gabriel was it, who, weary with waiting, un-
    happy and restless,
Sought in the Western wilds oblivion of self
    and of sorrow.   ₈₃₅
Swiftly they glided along, close under the lee°
    of the island,

But by the opposite bank, and behind a screen
    of palmettos,
So that they saw not the boat, where it lay
    concealed in the willows;
All undisturbed by the dash of their oars, and
    unseen, were the sleepers.
Angel of God was there none to awaken the
    slumbering maiden.   810
Swiftly they glided away, like the shade of a
    cloud on the prairie.
After the sound of their oars on the tholes°
    had died in the distance,
As from a magic trance the sleepers awoke,
    and the maiden
Said with a sigh to the friendly priest, "O
    Father Felician!
Something says in my heart that near me
    Gabriel wanders.   845
Is it a foolish dream, an idle and vague super-
    stition?
Or has an angel passed, and revealed the truth
    to my spirit?"
Then, with a blush, she added, "Alas for my
    credulous° fancy!
Unto ears like thine such words as these have
    no meaning."
But made answer the reverend man, and he
    smiled as he answered, —   850
"Daughter, thy words are not idle; nor are
    they to me without meaning,

Feeling is deep and still; and the word that
    floats on the surface
Is as the tossing buoy, that betrays where the
    anchor is hidden.
Therefore trust to thy heart, and to what the
    world calls illusions.°
Gabriel truly is near thee; for not far away
    to the southward,   855
On the banks of the Têche,° are the towns of
    St. Maur° and St. Martin.°
There the long-wandering bride shall be given
    again to her bridegroom,
There the long-absent pastor regain his flock
    and his sheepfold.
Beautiful is the land, with its prairies and for-
    ests of fruit-trees;
Under the feet a garden of flowers, and the
    bluest of heavens   860
Bending above, and resting its dome on the
    walls of the forest.
They who dwell there have named it the Eden
    of Louisiana!"

    With these words of cheer they arose and
    continued their journey.
Softly the evening came. The sun from the
    western horizon
Like a magician extended his golden wand o'er
    the landscape;   865

Twinkling vapors arose; and sky and water and
    forest

Seemed all on fire at the touch, and melted
    and mingled together.

Hanging between two skies, a cloud with edges
    of silver,

Floated the boat, with its dripping oars, on the
    motionless water.

Filled was Evangeline's heart with inexpres-
    sible sweetness.   870

Touched by the magic spell, the sacred foun-
    tains of feeling

Glowed with the light of love, as the skies and
    waters around her.

Then from a neighboring thicket the mocking-
    bird, wildest of singers,

Swinging aloft on a willow spray that hung
    o'er the water,

Shook from his little throat such floods of
    delirious music,   875

That the whole air and the woods and the
    waves seemed silent to listen.

Plaintive at first were the tones and sad; then
    soaring to madness·

Seemed they to follow or guide the revel of
    frenzied Bacchantes.°

Single notes were then heard, in sorrowful,
    low lamentation;

Till, having gathered them all, he flung them
    abroad in derision,   880

As when, after a storm, a gust of wind through
    the tree-tops
Shakes down the rattling rain in a crystal
    shower on the branches.
With such a prelude as this, and hearts that
    throbbed with emotion,
Slowly they entered the Têche, where it flows
    through the green Opelousas,
And, through the amber air, above the crest
    of the woodland,   885
Saw the column of smoke that arose from a
    neighboring dwelling;—
Sounds of a horn they heard, and the distant
    lowing of cattle.

III

Near to the bank of the river, o'ershadowed
    by oaks, from whose branches
Garlands of Spanish moss and of mystic mistle-
    toe flaunted,
Such as the Druids cut down with golden
    hatchets at Yule-tide,°   890
Stood, secluded and still, the house of the
    herdsman. A garden
Girded it round about with a belt of luxuriant
    blossoms,
Filling the air with fragrance. The house itself
    was of timbers

Hewn from the cypress-tree, and carefully fitted
    together.

Large and low was the roof; and on slender
    columns supported,   895

Rose-wreathed, vine-encircled, a broad and
    spacious veranda,

Haunt of the humming-bird and the bee, ex-
    tended around it.

At each end of the house, amid the flowers of
    the garden,

Stationed the dove-cots were, as love's perpet-
    ual symbol,

Scenes of endless wooing, and endless conten-
    tions of rivals.   900

Silence reigned o'er the place. The line of
    shadow and sunshine

Ran near the tops of the trees; but the house
    itself was in shadow,

And from its chimney-top, ascending and
    slowly expanding

Into the evening air, a thin blue column of
    smoke rose.

In the rear of the house, from the garden gate,
    ran a pathway   905

Through the great groves of oak to the skirts
    of the limitless prairie,

Into whose sea of flowers the sun was slowly
    descending.

Full in his track of light, like ships with
    shadowy canvas

Hanging loose from their spars in a motionless
    calm in the tropics,
Stood a cluster of trees, with tangled cordage of
    grape-vines.   910

Just where the woodlands met the flowery
    surf° of the prairie,
Mounted upon his horse, with Spanish saddle
    and stirrups,
Sat a herdsman, arrayed in gaiters and doublet
    of deerskin.
Broad and brown was the face that from under
    the Spanish sombrero
Gazed on the peaceful scene, with the lordly
    look of its master   915
Round about him were numberless herds of
    kine, that were grazing
Quietly in the meadows, and breathing the va-
    pory freshness
That uprose from the river, and spread itself
    over the landscape.
Slowly lifting the horn that hung at his side,
    and expanding
Fully his broad, deep chest, he blew a blast,
    that resounded   920
Wildly and sweet and far, through the still
    damp air of the evening.
Suddenly out of the grass the long white horns
    of the cattle

Rose like flakes of foam on the adverse currents of ocean.

Silent a moment they gazed, then bellowing rushed o'er the prairie,

And the whole mass became a cloud, a shade in the distance. 925

Then, as the herdsman turned to the house, through the gate of the garden

Saw he the forms of the priest and the maiden advancing to meet him.

Suddenly down from his horse he sprang in amazement, and forward

Rushed with extended arms and exclamations of wonder;

When they beheld his face, they recognized Basil the blacksmith. 930

Hearty his welcome was, as he led his guests to the garden.

There in an arbor of roses with endless question and answer

Gave they vent to their hearts, and renewed their friendly embraces,

Laughing and weeping by turns, or sitting silent and thoughtful.

Thoughtful, for Gabriel came not; and now dark doubts and misgivings 935

Stole o'er the maiden's heart; and Basil, somewhat embarrassed,

Broke the silence and said, "If you came by the Atchafalaya,

How have you nowhere encountered my
    Gabriel's boat on the bayous?"
Over Evangeline's face at the words of Basil a
    shade passed.
Tears came into her eyes, and she said, with
    a tremulous accent,   940
"Gone? is Gabriel gone?" and, concealing her
    face on his shoulder,
All her o'erburdened heart gave way, and she
    wept and lamented.
Then the good Basil said,—and his voice grew
    blithe as he said it,—
"Be of good cheer, my child; it is only to-day
    he departed.
Foolish boy! he has left me alone with my
    herds and my horses.   945
Moody and restless grown, and tried and
    troubled, his spirit
Could no longer endure the calm of this quiet
    existence.
Thinking ever of thee, uncertain and sorrow-
    ful ever,
Ever silent, or speaking only of thee and his
    troubles,
He at length had become so tedious to men
    and to maidens,   950
Tedious even to me, that at length I bethought
    me, and sent him
Unto the town of Adayes° to trade for mules
    with the Spaniards.

Thence he will follow the Indian trails to the
    Ozark Mountains,°
Hunting for furs in the forests, on rivers trap-
    ping the beaver.
Therefore be of good cheer; we will follow
    the fugitive lover;   955
He is not far on his way, and the Fates and
    the streams are against him.
Up and away to-morrow, and through the
    red dew of the morning
We will follow him fast, and bring him back
    to his prison."

Then glad voices were heard, and up from
    the banks of the river,
Borne aloft on his comrades' arms, came
    Michael the fiddler.   960
Long under Basil's roof had he lived like a
    god on Olympus,°
Having no other care than dispensing music to
    mortals.
Far renowned was he for his silver locks and
    his fiddle.
"Long live Michael," they cried, "our brave
    Acadian minstrel!"
As they bore him aloft in triumphal procession;
    and straightway   965
Father Felician advanced with Evangeline,
    greeting the old man

Kindly and oft, and recalling the past, while
    Basil, enraptured,
Hailed with hilarious joy his old companions
    and gossips,
Laughing loud and long, and embracing moth-
    ers and daughters.
Much they marvelled to see the wealth of the
    ci-devant° blacksmith,   970
All his domains and his herds, and his patriar-
    chal° demeanor;
Much they marvelled to hear his tales of the
    soil and the climate,
And of the prairies, whose numberless herds
    were his who would take them;°
Each one thought in his heart, that he, too,
    would go and do likewise.
Thus they ascended the steps, and, crossing the
    breezy veranda,   975
Entered the hall of the house, where already
    the supper of Basil
Waited his late return; and they rested and
    feasted together.

Over the joyous feast the sudden darkness
    descended.
All was silent without, and, illuming the land-
    scape with silver,
Fair rose the dewy moon and the myriad stars;
    but within doors,   980

Brighter than these, shone the faces of friends
    in the glimmering lamplight.

Then from his station aloft, at the head of the
    table, the herdsman

Poured forth his heart and his wine together
    in endless profusion.

Lighting his pipe, that was filled with sweet
    Natchitoches tobacco,

Thus he spake to his guests, who listened, and
    smiled as they listened:—   985

"Welcome once more, my friends, who long
    have been friendless and homeless,

Welcome once more to a home, that is better
    perchance than the old one!

Here no hungry winter congeals our blood like
    the rivers;

Here no stony ground provokes the wrath of
    the farmer;

Smoothly the ploughshare runs through the
    soil, as a keel through the water.   990

All the year round the orange-groves are in
    blossom; and grass grows

More in a single night than a whole Canadian
    summer.

Here, too, numberless herds run wild and un-
    claimed in the prairies;

Here, too, lands may be had for the asking,
    and forests of timber

With a few blows of the axe are hewn and
    framed into houses.   995

Far down the Beautiful River, . . .
Floated a cumbrous boat, that was rowed by
Acadian boatmen.

After your houses are built, and your fields
    are yellow with harvests,

No King George of England shall drive you
    away from your homesteads,

Burning your dwellings and barns, and steal-
    ing your farms and your cattle."

Speaking these words, he blew a wrathful cloud
    from his nostrils,

While his huge, brown hand came thundering
    down on the table,   1000

So that the guests all started; and Father Feli-
    cian, astounded,

Suddenly paused, with a pinch of snuff half-
    way to his nostrils.

But the brave Basil resumed, and his words
    were milder and gayer:—

"Only beware of the fever, my friends, beware
    of the fever!

For it is not, like that of our cold Acadian
    climate,   1005

Cured° by wearing a spider hung round one's
    neck in a nutshell!"

Then there were voices heard at the door, and
    footsteps approaching

Sounded upon the stairs and the floor of the
    breezy veranda.

It was the neighboring Creoles° and small
    Acadian planters,

Who had been summoned all to the house of
    Basil the Herdsman.   1010

Merry the meeting was of ancient comrades
and neighbors:
Friend clasped friend in his arms; and they
who before were as strangers,
Meeting in exile, became straightway as friends
to each other,
Drawn by the gentle bond of a common coun-
try together.
But in the neighboring hall a strain of music,
proceeding   1015
From the accordant strings .of Michael's melo-
dious fiddle,
Broke up all further speech. Away, like chil-
dren delighted,
All things forgotten beside, they gave them-
selves to the maddening
Whirl of the giddy dance, as it swept and
swayed to the music,
Dreamlike, with beaming eyes and the rush of
fluttering garments.   1020

Meanwhile, apart, at the head of the hall,
the priest and the herdsman
Sat, conversing together of past and present
and future;
While Evangeline stood like one entranced, for
within her
Olden memories rose, and loud in the midst of
the music

Heard she the sound of the sea,° and an irre-
    pressible sadness   1025
Came o'er her heart, and unseen she stole
    forth into the garden.
Beautiful was the night. Behind the black wall
    of the forest,
Tipping its summit with silver, arose the moon.
    On the river
Fell here and there through the branches a
    tremulous gleam of the moonlight,
Like the sweet thoughts of love on a darkened
    and devious spirit.   1030
Nearer and round about her, the manifold
    flowers of the garden
Poured out their souls in odors, that were their
    prayers and confessions
Unto the night, as it went its way, like a silent
    Carthusian.°
Fuller of fragrance than they, and as heavy
    with shadows and night-dews,
Hung the heart of the maiden. The calm and
    the magical moonlight   1035
Seemed to inundate her soul with indefinable
    longings,
As, through the garden gate, and beneath the
    shade of the oak-trees,
Passed she along the path to the edge of the
    measureless prairie.
Silent it lay, with a silvery haze upon it, and
    fireflies

Gleaming and floating away in mingled and
    infinite numbers. 1040
Over her head the stars, the thoughts of God
    in the heavens,°
Shone on the eyes of man, who had ceased to
    marvel and worship,
Save when a blazing comet was seen on the
    walls of that temple,
As if ·a hand had appeared and written upon
    them, "Upharsin."°
And the soul of ·the maiden, between the stars
    and ·the fire-flies, 1045
Wandered alone, and she cried, "O Gabriel!
    O my beloved!
Art thou so near unto me, and yet I cannot
    behold thee?
Art thou so near unto me, and yet thy voice
    does not reach me?
Ah! how often thy feet have trod this path to
    the prairie!
Ah! how often thine eyes have looked on the
    woodlands around me! 1050
Ah! how often beneath this oak, returning from
    labor,
Thou hast lain down to rest, and to dream
    of me in thy slumbers!
When shall these eyes behold, these arms be
    folded about thee?"
Loud and sudden and near the note of a whip-
    poorwill sounded

Like a flute in the woods; and anon, through
the neighboring thickets,   1055
Farther and farther away it floated and dropped
into silence.
"Patience!" whispered the oaks from oracular
caverns° of darkness;
And, from the moonlit meadow, a sigh re-
sponded, "To-morrow!"

Bright rose the sun next day; and all the
flowers of the garden
Bathed his shining feet with their tears, and
anointed his tresses   1060
With the delicious balm that they bore in their
vases of crystal.°
"Farewell!" said the priest, as he stood at the
shadowy threshold;
"See that you bring us the Prodigal Son from
his fasting and famine,
And, too, the Foolish Virgin, who slept when
the bridegroom was coming."
"Farewell," answered the maiden, and, smil-
ing, with Basil descended   1065
Down to the river's brink, where the boatmen
already were waiting.
Thus beginning their journey with morning,
and sunshine, and gladness,
Swiftly they followed the flight of him who
was speeding before them,

Blown by the blast of fate like a dead leaf over
    the desert.
Not that day, nor the next, nor yet the day
    that succeeded,   1070
Found they the trace of his course, in lake or
    forest or river,
Nor, after many days, had they found him;
    but vague and uncertain
Rumors alone were their guides through a wild
    and desolate country;
Till, at the little inn of the Spanish town of
    Adayes,
Weary and worn, they alighted, and learned
    from the garrulous° landlord   1075
That on the day before, with horses and guides
    and companions,
Gabriel left the village, and took the road of the
    prairies.

IV

Far in the West there lies a desert land,
    where the mountains
Lift, through perpetual snows, their lofty and
    luminous summits.
Down from their jagged, deep ravines, where
    the gorge, like a gateway.   1080
Opens a passage rude to the wheels of the
    emigrant's wagon,
Westward the Oregon° flows and the Walle-
    way° and Owyhee.°

Eastward, with devious course, among the
    Wind-river Mountains,°
Through the Sweet-water Valley° precipitate
    leaps the Nebraska;
And to the south, from Fontaine-qui-bout° and
    the Spanish sierras,°   1085
Fretted with sands and rocks, and swept by
    the wind of the desert,
Numberless torrents, with ceaseless sound, de-
    scend to the ocean,
Like the great chords of a harp, in loud and
    solemn vibrations.
Spreading between these streams are the won-
    drous, beautiful prairies,
Billowy bays of grass ever rolling in shadow
    and sunshine,   1090
Bright with luxuriant clusters of roses and pur-
    ple amorphas.
Over them wandered the buffalo herds, and the
    elk and the roebuck;
Over them wandered the wolves, and herds of
    riderless horses;
Fires that blast and blight, and winds that are
    weary with travel;
Over them wander the scattered tribes of Ish-
    mael's children,°   1095
Staining the desert with blood; and above their
    terrible war-trails
Circles and sails aloft, on pinions majestic, the
    vulture,

Like the implacable soul of a chieftain slaugh-
    tered in battle,
By invisible stairs ascending and scaling the
    heavens.
Here and there rise smokes from the camps
    of these savage marauders;   1100
Here and there rise groves from the margins
    of swift-running rivers;
And the grim, taciturn° bear, the anchorite°
    monk of the desert,
Climbs down their dark ravines to dig for roots
    by the brook-side,
And over all is the sky, the clear and the crys-
    talline heaven,
Like the protecting hand of God inverted above
    them.   1105

  Into this wonderful land, at the base of the
    Ozark Mountains,°
Gabriel far had entered, with hunters and
    trappers behind him.
Day after day, with their Indian guides, the
    maiden and Basil
Followed his flying steps, and thought each
    day to o'ertake him.
Sometimes they saw, or thought they saw, the
    smoke of his camp-fire   1110
Rise in the morning air from the distant plain;
    but at nightfall,

When they had reached the place, they found
    only embers and ashes.
And, though their hearts were sad at times and
    their bodies were weary,
Hope still guided them on, as the magic Fata
    Morgana°
Showed them her lakes of light, that retreated
    and vanished before them.   1115

Once, as they sat by their evening fire, there
    silently entered
Into their little camp an Indian woman, whose
    features
Wore deep traces of sorrow, and patience as
    great as her sorrow.
She was a Shawnee woman returning home to
    her people,
From the far-off hunting-grounds of the cruel
    Comanches,   1120
Where her Canadian husband, a coureur-des-
    bois, had been murdered.
Touched were their hearts at her story, and
    warmest and friendliest welcome
Gave they, with words of cheer, and she sat
    and feasted among them
On the buffalo-meat and the venison cooked
    on the embers.
But when their meal was done, and Basil and
    all his companions,   1125

Worn with the long day's march and the chase
    of the deer and the bison,
Stretched themselves on the ground, and slept
    where the quivering fire-light
Flashed on their swarthy cheeks, and their
    forms wrapped up in their blankets,
Then at the door of Evangeline's tent she sat
    and repeated
Slowly, with soft, low voice, and the charm
    of her Indian accent,   1130
All the tale of her love, with its pleasures, and
    pains, and reverses.
Much Evangeline wept at the tale, and to know
    that another
Hapless heart like her own had loved and had
    been disappointed.
Moved to the depths of her soul by pity and
    woman's compassion,
Yet in her sorrow pleased that one who had
    suffered was near her,   1135
She in turn related her love and all its dis-
    asters.
Mute with wonder the Shawnee sat, and when
    she had ended
Still was mute; but at length, as if a mysterious
    horror
Passed through her brain, she spake, and re-
    peated the tale of the Mowis°;
Mowis, the bridegroom of snow, who won and
    wedded a maiden,   1140

But, when the morning came, arose and passed
    from the wigwam,
Fading and melting away and dissolving into
    the sunshine,
Till she beheld him no more, though she fol-
    lowed far into the forest.
Then, in those sweet, low tones, that seemed
    like a weird incantation,
Told she the tale of the fair Lilinau, who was
    wooed by a phantom,   1145
That through the pines o'er her father's lodge,
    in the hush of the twilight,
Breathed like the evening wind, and whispered
    love to the maiden,
Till she followed his green and waving plume
    through the forest,
And nevermore returned, nor was seen again
    by her people.
Silent with wonder and strange surprise, Evan-
    geline listened   1150
To the soft flow of her magical words, till the
    region around her
Seemed like enchanted ground, and her swarthy
    guest the enchantress.
Slowly over the tops of the Ozark Mountains
    the moon rose,
Lighting the little tent, and with a mysterious
    splendor
Touching the sombre leaves, and embracing and
    filling the woodland.   1155

With a delicious sound the brook rushed by,
    and the branches
Swayed and sighed overhead in scarcely audible
    whispers.
Filled with the thoughts of love was Evan-
    geline's heart, but a secret,
Subtile sense crept in of pain and indefinite
    terror,
As the cold, poisonous snake creeps into the
    nest of the swallow.   1160
It was no earthly fear. A breath from the region
    of spirits
Seemed to float in the air of night; and she
    felt for a moment
That, like the Indian maid, she, too, was pur-
    suing a phantom.
With this thought she slept, and the fear and
    the phantom had vanished.

Early upon the morrow the march was re-
    sumed, and the Shawnee   1165
Said, as they journeyed along,—"On the west-
    ern slope of these mountains
Dwells in his little village the Black Robe°
    chief of the Mission.
Much he teaches the people, and tells them of
    Mary and Jesus,
Loud laugh their hearts with joy, and weep
    with pain, as they hear him."

Then, with a sudden and secret emotion, Evan-
    geline answered,   1170
"Let us go to the Mission, for there good tidings
    await us!"
Thither they turned their steeds; and behind a
    spur of the mountains,
Just as the sun went down, they heard a mur-
    mur of voices,
And in a meadow green and broad, by the
    bank of a river,
Saw the tents of the Christians, the tents of
    the Jesuit° Mission.   1175
Under a towering oak, that stood in the midst
    of the village,
Knelt the Black Robe chief with his children.
    A crucifix fastened
High on the trunk of the tree, and overshad-
    owed by grapevines,
Looked with its agonized face on the multitude
    kneeling beneath it.
This was their rural chapel. Aloft, through the
    intricate arches   1180
Of its aerial roof, arose the chant of their
    vespers,°
Mingling its notes with the soft susurrus° and
    sighs of the branches.
Silent, with heads uncovered, the travellers,
    nearer approaching,
Knelt on the swarded° floor, and joined in the
    evening devotions.

But when the service was done, and the bene-
   diction had fallen   1185
Forth from the hands of the priest, like seed
   from the hands of the sower,
Slowly the reverend man advanced to the
   strangers, and bade them
Welcome; and when they replied, he smiled
   with benignant expression,
Hearing the homelike sounds of his mother-
   tongue in the forest,
And, with words of kindness, conducted them
   into his wigwam.   1190
There upon mats and skins they reposed, and
   on cakes of the maize-ear
Feasted, and slaked their thirst from the water-
   gourd of the teacher.
Soon was their story told; and the priest with
   solemnity answered:—
"Not six suns have risen and set since Gabriel,
   seated
On this mat by my side, where now the maiden
   reposes,   1195
Told me this same sad tale; then arose and
   continued his journey!"
Soft was the voice of the priest, and he spake
   with an accent of kindness;
But on Evangeline's heart fell his words as in
   winter the snow-flakes
Fall into some lone nest from which the birds
   have departed.

"Far to the north he has gone," continued the
    priest; "but in autumn,   1200
When the chase is done, will return again to the
    Mission."
Then Evangeline said, and her voice was meek
    and submissive,
"Let me remain with thee, for my soul is sad
    and afflicted."
So seemed it wise and well unto all; and be-
    times on the morrow,
Mounting his Mexican steed, with his Indian
    guides and companions,   1205
Homeward Basil returned, and Evangeline
    stayed at the Mission.

  Slowly, slowly, slowly the days succeeded
    each other,—
Days and weeks and months; and the fields
    of maize that were springing
Green from the ground when a stranger she
    came, now waving above her,
Lifted their slender shafts, with leaves inter-
    lacing, and forming   1210
Cloisters for mendicant° crows and granaries
    pillaged by squirrels.
Then in the golden weather the maize was
    husked, and the maidens
Blushed at each blood-red ear, for that be-
    tokened a lover,

But at the crooked laughed, and called it a
    thief in the corn-field.
Even the blood-red ear to Evangeline brought
    not her lover.   1215
"Patience!" the priest would say; "have faith,
    and thy prayer will be answered!
Look at this vigorous plant that lifts its head
    from the meadow,
See how its leaves are turned to the north, as
    true as the magnet;
This is the compass-flower,° that the finger of
    God has planted
Here in the houseless wild, to direct the trav-
    eller's journey   1220
Over the sea-like, pathless, limitless waste of
    the desert.
Such in the soul of man is faith. The blossoms
    of passion,
Gay and luxuriant flowers, are brighter and
    fuller of fragrance,
But they beguile us, and lead us astray, and
    their odor is deadly.
Only this humble plant can guide us here, and
    hereafter   1225
Crown us with asphodel° flowers, that are wet
    with the dews of nepenthe." °

So came the autumn, and passed, and the
    winter—yet Gabriel came not;

Blossomed the opening spring, and the notes of
the robin and bluebird

Sounded sweet upon wold° and in wood, yet
Gabriel came not.

But on the breath of the summer winds a rumor
was wafted   1230

Sweeter than song of bird, or hue or odor of
blossom.

Far to the north and east, it said, in the Michigan
forests,

Gabriel had his lodge by the banks of the
Saginaw River.

And, with returning guides, that sought the
lakes of St. Lawrence,

Saying a sad farewell, Evangeline went from
the Mission.   1235

When over weary ways, by long and perilous
marches,

She had attained at length the depths of the
Michigan forests,

Found she the hunter's lodge deserted and
fallen to ruin!

Thus did the long sad years glide on, and
in seasons and places

Divers° and distant far was seen the wandering
maiden:—   1240

Now in the Tents of Grace° of the meek
Moravian Missions,

Now in the noisy camps and the battle-fields
    of the army,
Now in secluded hamlets, in towns and
    populous cities.
Like a phantom she came, and passed away un-
    remembered.
Fair was she and young, when in hope began
    the long journey;   1245
Faded was she and old, when in disappoint-
    ment it ended.
Each succeeding year stole something away
    from her beauty,
Leaving behind it, broader and deeper, the
    gloom and the shadow.
Then there appeared and spread faint streaks
    of gray o'er her forehead,
Dawn of another life, that broke o'er her
    earthly horizon,   1250
As in the eastern sky the first faint streaks of
    the morning.

V

In that delightful land which is washed by
    the Delaware's waters,
Guarding in sylvan° shades the name of Penn
    the apostle,
Stands on the banks of its beautiful stream the
    city he founded.

There all the air is balm, and the peach is the
    emblem of beauty, ₁₂₅₅
And the streets still reëcho the names of the
    trees of the forest,
As if they fain would appease the Dryads°
    whose haunts they molested.
There from the troubled sea had Evangeline
    landed, an exile,
Finding among the children of Penn a home
    and a country.
There old René Leblanc had died; and when
    he departed, ₁₂₆₀
Saw at his side only one of all his hundred
    descendants.
Something at least there was in the friendly
    streets of the city,
Something that spake to her heart, and made
    her no longer a stranger;
And her ear was pleased with the Thee and
    Thou of the Quakers,
For it recalled the past, the old Acadian coun-
    try, ₁₂₆₅
Where all men were equal, and all were broth-
    ers and sisters.
So, when the fruitless search, the disappointed
    endeavor,
Ended, to recommence no more upon earth,
    uncomplaining,
Thither, as leaves to the light, were turned her
    thoughts and her footsteps.

As from a mountain's top the rainy mists of
    the morning   1270
Roll away, and afar we behold the landscape
    below us,
Sun-illumined, with shining rivers and cities
    and hamlets,
So fell the mists from her mind, and she saw
    the world far below her,
Dark no longer, but all illumined with love;
    and the pathway
Which she had climbed so far, lying smooth
    and fair in the distance.   1275
Gabriel was not forgotten. Within her heart
    was his image,
Clothed in the beauty of love and youth, as
    last she beheld him,
Only more beautiful made by his death-like
    silence and absence.
Into her thoughts of him time entered not,
    for it was not.
Over him years had no power; he was not
    changed, but transfigured;   1280
He had become to her heart as one who is dead
    and not absent;
Patience and abnegation° of self, and devotion
    to others,
This was the lesson a life of trial and sorrow
    had taught her.
So was her love diffused, but, like to some
    odorous spices,

Suffered no waste nor loss, though filling the
air with aroma.   1285
Other hope had she none, nor wish in life, but
to follow,
Meekly, with reverent steps, the sacred feet
of her Saviour.
Thus many years she lived as a Sister of
Mercy; frequenting
Lonely and wretched roofs in the crowded
lanes of the city,
Where distress and want concealed themselves
from the sunlight,   1290
Where disease and sorrow in garrets languished
neglected.
Night after night when the world was asleep,
as the watchman repeated
Loud, through the gusty streets, that all was
well in the city,
High at some lonely window he saw the light
of her taper.
Day after day, in the gray of the dawn, as
slow through the suburbs   1295
Plodded the German farmer, with flowers and
fruits for the market,
Met he that meek, pale face, returning home
from its watchings.

Then it came to pass that a pestilence° fell
on the city,

Presaged° by wondrous signs, and mostly by
    flocks of wild pigeons,

Darkening the sun in their flight, with naught
    in their craws but an acorn.   1300

And, as the tides of the sea arise in the month
    of September,

Flooding some silver stream, till it spreads to
    a lake in the meadow,

So death flooded life, and, o'erflowing its
    natural margin,

Spread to a brackish° lake the silver stream
    of existence.

Wealth had no power to bribe, nor beauty
    to charm, the oppressor;   1305

But all perished alike beneath the scourge of
    his anger;—

Only, alas! the poor, who had neither friends
    nor attendants,

Crept away to die in the almshouse,° home of
    the homeless.

Then in the suburbs it stood, in the midst of
    meadows and woodlands;—

Now the city surrounds it; but still, with its
    gateway and wicket   1310

Meek, in the midst of splendor, its humble
    walls seem to echo

Softly the words of the Lord: "The poor ye
    always have with you."

Thither, by night and by day, came the Sister
    of Mercy. The dying

Looked up into her face, and thought, indeed,
  to behold there
Gleams of celestial light encircle her forehead
  with splendor,   1315
Such as the artist paints o'er the brows of
  saints and apostles,
Or such as hangs by night o'er a city seen at
  a distance.
Unto their eyes it seemed the lamps of the city
  celestial,
Into whose shining gates ere long their spirits
  would enter.

  Thus, on a Sabbath morn, through the streets,
    deserted and silent,   1320
Wending her quiet way, she entered the door
  of the almshouse.
Sweet on the summer air was the odor of
  flowers in the garden;
And she paused on her way to gather the fair-
  est among them,
That the dying once more might rejoice in
  their fragrance and beauty.
Then, as she mounted the stairs to the cor-
  ridors, cooled by the east-wind,   1325
Distant and soft on her ear fell the chimes from
  the belfry of Christ Church,
While, intermingled with these, across the
  meadows were wafted

Sounds of psalms, that were sung by the
    Swedes° in their church at Wicaco.

Soft as descending wings fell the calm of the
    hour on her spirit;

Something within her said, "At length thy trials
    are ended";   1330

And, with light in her looks, she entered the
    chambers of sickness.

Noiselessly moved about the assiduous,° care-
    ful attendants,

Moistening the feverish lip, and the aching
    brow, and in silence

Closing the sightless eyes of the dead, and
    concealing their faces,

Where on their pallets° they lay, like drifts
    of snow by the roadside.   1335

Many a languid head, upraised as Evangeline
    entered,

Turned on its pillow of pain to gaze while she
    passed, for her presence

Fell on their hearts like a ray of the sun on the
    walls of a prison.

And, as she looked around, she saw how Death,
    the consoler,

Laying his hand upon many a heart, had healed
    it forever.   1340

Many familiar forms had disappeared in the
    night time;

Vacant their places were, or filled already by
    strangers.

Suddenly, as if arrested by fear or a feeling
    of wonder,
Still she stood, with her colorless lips apart,
    while a shudder
Ran through her frame, and, forgotten, the
    flowerets dropped from her fingers,   1345
And from her eyes and cheeks the light and
    bloom of the morning.
Then there escaped from her lips a cry of such
    terrible anguish,
That the dying heard it, and started up from
    their pillows.
On the pallet before her was stretched the form
    of an old man.
Long, and thin, and gray were the locks that
    shaded his temples;   1350
But, as he lay in the morning light, his face
    for a moment
Seemed to assume once more the forms of its
    earlier manhood;
So are wont to be changed the faces of those
    who are dying.
Hot and red on his lips still burned the flush
    of the fever,
As if life, like the Hebrew,° with blood had
    besprinkled its portals,   1355
That the Angel of Death might see the sign,
    and pass over.
Motionless, senseless, dying, he lay, and his
    spirit exhausted

Seemed to be sinking down through infinite
    depths in the darkness,

Darkness of slumber and death, forever sink-
    ing and sinking.

Then through those realms of shade, in multi-
    plied reverberations,   1360

Heard he that cry of pain, and through the
    hush that succeeded

Whispered a gentle voice, in accents tender
    and saint-like,

"Gabriel! O my beloved!" and died away into
    silence.

Then he beheld, in a dream, once more the
    home of his childhood;

Green Acadian meadows, with sylvan rivers
    among them,   1365

Village, and mountain, and woodlands; and,
    walking under their shadow,

As in the days of her youth, Evangeline rose
    in his vision.

Tears came into his eyes; and as slowly he
    lifted his eyelids,

Vanished the vision away, but Evangeline
    knelt by his bedside.

Vainly he strove to whisper her name, for the
    accents unuttered   1370

Died on his lips, and their motion revealed
    what his tongue would have spoken.

Vainly he strove to rise; and Evangeline,
    kneeling beside him,

Whispered a gentle voice, in accents tender and saintlike
"Gabriel! O my beloved!" . . .

Kissed his dying lips, and laid his head on her
    bosom.
Sweet was the light of his eyes; but it sud-
    denly sank into darkness,
As when a lamp is blown out by a gust of wind
    at a casement.   1375

All was ended now, the hope, and the fear,
    and the sorrow,
All the aching of heart, the restless, unsatisfied
    longing,
All the dull, deep pain, and constant anguish
    of patience!
And, as she pressed once more the lifeless head
    to her bosom,
Meekly she bowed her own, and murmured,
    "Father, I thank thee!"   1380

Still stands the forest primeval; but far
    away from its shadow,
Side by side, in their nameless graves, the
    lovers are sleeping.
Under the humble walls of the little Catholic
    churchyard,
In the heart of the city, they lie, unknown
    and unnoticed.
Daily the tides of life go ebbing and flowing
    beside them,   1385

Thousands of throbbing hearts, where theirs
are at rest and forever,
Thousands of aching brains, where theirs no
longer are busy,
Thousands of toiling hands, where theirs have
ceased from their labors,
Thousands of weary feet, where theirs have
completed their journey!

Still stands the forest primeval°; but under
the shade of its branches   1390
Dwells another race, with other customs and
language.
Only along the shore of the mournful and
misty Atlantic
Linger a few Acadian peasants, whose fathers
from exile
Wandered back to their native land to die in
its bosom.
In the fisherman's cot the wheel and the loom
are still busy;   1395
Maidens still wear their Norman caps and
their kirtles of homespun,
And by the evening fire repeat Evangeline's
story,
While from its rocky caverns the deep-voiced,
neighboring ocean
Speaks, and in accents disconsolate answers
the wail of the forest.

NOTES

LINE 1. **primeval:** belonging to the first age; very ancient.

l. 3. **Druids:** priests of the Celts, the earliest inhabitants of Britain and France. Groves of oak were the chosen retreat of the Druids. What grew on that tree was thought to be a gift from heaven, more especially the mistletoe. When thus found, the latter was cut with a golden knife by a priest clad in a white robe, and two white bulls were sacrificed on the spot. The Druids called the mistletoe "all heal." Compare *mystic mistletoe*, l. 889. **eld:** age, antiquity. A native English word. A.-S. yldo, derived from the adjective eald, old. The word *eld* is no longer used except in poetry, though we still employ the comparative *elder*.

l. 4. **harpers.** Now less common than *harpist*. **Hoar.** Hoary or white with age. Note how frequently alliteration is employed in this poem.

l. 8. **roe:** a variety of deer.

l. 11. **Darkened,** etc. Show how this line explains the comparison made in the preceding line.

l. 15. **Grand-Pré.** The name means *great meadow*. See ll. 22-23.

l. 19. **Acadie.** The country now called Nova Scotia was discovered by Sebastian Cabot, in 1497. Later Verrazani took possession of the territory in the name of the King of France. In early records it is variously called Cadie, Arcadia, Accadia, and L'Acadie; the name was probably of Indian derivation.

l. 20. **Minas.** That is, *Les Mines,* from the copper mines said to lie about it.

l. 29. **Blomidon.** A rocky cape, to the north of Grand-Pré.

l. 34. **Normandy.** The province in France from which many of the Acadians came. The picture here presented is familiar to visitors to the Normandy of today. **The Henries.** The French kings Henry III and Henry IV (1574-1610), in whose reigns Acadia was settled.

l. 35. **dormer-windows:** vertical windows projecting from a sloping roof.

l. 39. **kirtles:** close-fitting gowns worn by Norman peasants.

l. 40. **distaffs:** staves used to hold bunches of wool, flax, etc., in spinning.

l. 41. **gossiping.** Is this word well-chosen? Why?

l. 48. **Anon:** soon.

l. 49. **Angelus:** a bell sounded at morning, noon, and evening, when a service is held to commemorate the incarnation of Christ. See the famous painting by Millet.

l. 54. **envy.** Do you agree with the poet that envy is peculiarly the vice of republics?

l. 62. **Stalworth.** A Middle English form, corrupted in Modern English to *stalwart.* A.-S. *staelwyre,* serviceable. The word teaches something about Anglo-Saxon manners, inasmuch as by derivation it means *good or worthy at stealing,* hence *brave.* **Winters.** What common figure in this word? Compare *summers,* l. 65. Notice how the figures are developed.

l. 68. **kine:** An old plural of *cow.*

l. 70. **sooth:** An old word meaning *truth,* now used only in poetry.

l. 72. **hyssop:** a plant, the twigs of which were used in Hebrew times in the ceremony of purification.

l. 74. **chaplet of beads:** a rosary, or string of beads, representing prayers used in the Roman service; **missal:** the Roman Catholic mass-book.

l. 87. **penthouse:** originally a shed or roof, usually sloping from a wall or a building.

l. 88. **Such as the traveller sees.** The reference here is to the wayside shrines erected in Catholic countries, for the convenience of travelers.

l. 93. **wains.** wagons. **antique:** old-fashioned.

l. 94. **seraglio:** harem.

l. 96. **Penitent Peter.** See "Matthew" XXVI.

l. 99. **corn-loft.** Here the word *corn* doubtless means wheat or other small grain, as in the *Bible*, or in England today.

l. 102. **mutation:** change, an appropriate theme for the song of a weathercock.

l. 108. **by the darkness befriended.** Why does the timid suitor feel that the darkness is a friend?

l. 117. **For since the birth of time.** Like many a village boy, Longfellow was always thrilled by a blacksmith shop. One of his best-known poems, "The Village Blacksmith," furnishes an interesting comparison with ll. 124-133. Possibly one reason for the prominence of the smith in ancient history is that he alone could make the tools, weapons, and armor that men could not do without. What do you know of Hephaestus and the Cyclops? of Vulcan? of Wieland? In the Anglo-Saxon poem *Beowulf*, a shirt-of-mail which one king sends as a gift to another is said to be "best of garments, the work of Wieland." Wayland Smith is a mysterious and very interesting character in Scott's *Kenilworth*, and in Kipling's *Puck of Pook's Hill*.

l. 122. **plain-song:** a chant, not extending beyond the compass of an octave.

l. 130. **smithy.** Both this word and its ally *stithy* have, unfortunately, been displaced in the common language by the cumbersome *blacksmith shop*.

l. 133. **they:** the sparks.

l. 139. **Lucky.** From early times this stone was regarded as a miraculous remedy.

l. 144. **Sunshine of Saint Eulalie.** Saint Eulalie's day is the 12th of February.

l. 149. **Scorpion:** The sun enters the sign Scorpio about October 23.

l. 153. **Jacob.** See "Genesis" XXXII.

ll. 154-157. **thick was the fur of the foxes.** Do you know any other signs that are believed to forecast the weather? Why were such signs felt to be very important in early times?

l. 159. **All-Saints.** All-Saints' day falls on November 1.

The summer of All-Saints would, then, correspond to our Indian summer.

l. 170. **the Persian.** The historian Herodotus says that Xerxes, in the course of his march through Asia Minor, found a beautiful plane-tree, with which he fell in love. He decorated it with jewels of gold and appointed a steward to attend it.

l. 180-183. **watch-dog.** What breed of dog do you judge this to be?

l. 184. **Regent:** ruler.

l. 187. **briny hay:** hay that grows in the salt-marshes by the sea.

l. 188. **fetlocks:** the tufted projections just above the hoofs.

ll. 193-194. Note how the ringing and hissing consonants imitate the sound of milking.

l. 205. **pewter:** an alloy of tin, formerly much used in the making of vessels and dishes. **dresser:** a cupboard or set of shelves to receive cooking utensils.

l. 223. **settle:** a high-backed seat or bench.

l. 233. **Gloomy forebodings of ill:** the first hint of evil. The student should watch for other forebodings throughout the story.

l. 234. **horseshoe.** A natural remark for Basil to make.

l. 240. **mandate:** command.

l. 249. **Louisburg,** etc. Louisburg was captured by the English and colonial troops under General Pepperell in 1745 (King George's War). Beau Sejour surrendered to the English in 1755. **Port Royal,** the first permanent settlement made by the French in America, was taken by the English in 1710; it was retained by the latter under the terms of the peace of 1713, and its name was changed to Annapolis Royal, in honor of Queen Anne.

l. 259. **contract:** a contract of betrothal, a formal engagement of marriage.

l. 261. **glebe:** soil. Note the delightful old custom here described.

l. 262. **inkhorn:** a portable case made of horn, for ink and writing instruments. In the days when few people were able to write, scholars and officials often bore ink-horns as necessary equipment.

l. 267. **notary:** a public officer, whose business is to acknowledge signatures of deeds, contracts, and other documents.

l. 272. **supernal:** celestial, heavenly. The use of this word gives a light touch of satire to the picture of the notary.

l. 280. **Loup-garou.** According to popular superstition the *loup-garou* or, in English, the *werwolf* (*man-wolf*), is a man who, because of a beastly appetite for human flesh, at times changes himself into a wolf, or who is changed against his will as a result of a charm or curse. This superstition has been prevalent in many parts of the world and from remote ages.

l. 287. **lore:** learning, here equivalent to the compound *folklore*.

l. 297. **irascible:** fiery, hot-tempered.

l. 306 ff. **Once in an ancient city.** This is an old Florentine story. (Scudder.)

l. 334. **parties.** Is the word correctly used here?

l. 335. **dower:** *dowry,* the money or property which a woman brings to her husband in marriage. The Acadians had little money, conducting most of their business affairs by barter; consequently the dower was "in flocks of sheep and in cattle." See also ll. 364-368.

l. 344. **draught-board:** checker-board, so called because the checkers are drawn from one square to another.

l. 346. **manoeuvre.** Now usually spelled *maneuver.*

l. 348. **embrasure:** the enlargement of a door or window on the inside of the wall, to give more room.

l. 354. **curfew.** The bell rung at an early hour of the evening (8 or 9 o'clock), to notify inhabitants of the village to extinguish lights and fires. The name is from the French: *couvre feu,* cover fire.

l. 376. **a feeling of sadness.** What value has this statement in the development of the story?

l. 381. **Ishmail wandered with Hagar.** "Genesis" XVI.

l. 386. **hundred hands.** Labor is compared to the hundred-handed giant Briareus.

l. 389. **jocund:** merry, gay.

l. 413. Old French songs with which Longfellow became acquainted in 1846.

l. 430. **commander:** Colonel Winslow; see Introduction.

l. 442. **solstice of summer:** about June 21. Look up this interesting word in a good dictionary.

l. 451. **cries and fierce imprecations . . . house of prayer.** Notice the effective contrast. *Imprecations* are *curses.*

l. 461. **chancel:** the part of a church that is reserved for the use of the priest.

l. 462. **mien:** bearing.

l. 466. **tocsin.** a signal bell. **alarum:** a Middle English form, still used in the dialects. It is a corruption of *alarm,* similar to the present vulgar pronunciation of ellum for elm, fillum for film.

l. 480. **contrition:** sorrow, repentance.

l. 484. **Ave Maria:** the *Hail Mary,* a prayer used in the Roman Catholic Church.

l. 485. **translated:** literally raised to heaven as Elijah was.

l. 492. **emblazoned:** literally, adorned with coats-of-arms; here, decorated in golden color.

l. 498: **ambrosial:** sweet, fragrant, like *ambrosia,* the food of the gods.

l. 507. **Prophet:** Moses. "Exodus" XXXIV. Like many other poets, Longfellow makes frequent allusions to the Bible. How many such references have occurred thus far?

l. 513. **gloomier grave of the living.** What is this?

l. 517 ff. **Sadly,** etc. Contrast Evangeline's situation with that of the previous evening.

l. 561. **spake.** Why not *spoke?*

l. 575. **refluent:** flowing back, ebbing.

l. 577. **waifs:** strays, homeless wanderers. **kelp:** a large brown seaweed.

l. 579. **leaguer:** the camp of a besieging army.

ll. 596-97. **Shipwrecked Paul.** A very apt reference. See "Acts" XXVII, XXVIII.

599-601. **Haggard . . . taken.** Is this an effective comparison?

l. 605. **Benedicite:** Bless you! One of the forms of salutation used by priests.

l. 615. **Titan-like.** In Greek mythology the Titans were a race of giants. Atlas, who supported the heavens, was a Titan.

l. 618. **roadstead:** an anchorage for ships. *Stead* is an old word for *place* or *spot,* still alive in *homestead.*

l. 621. **gleeds:** live coals.

l. 644. **oblivious:** forgetful.

l. 660. **dirges:** funeral songs or chants.

l. 668. **household gods:** traditions. The expression is a rendering of the Latin *Penates,* which was applied to the images of ancestors and protecting deities, to be found in every Roman home.

l. 674. **savannas:** plains, meadows.

l. 675. **Father of Waters:** The Mississippi.

l. 677. **mammoth.** Geologists have unearthed remains of mastodons and elephants in various parts of North America, from the Gulf to the Arctic circle.

l. 705. **Coureurs-des-bois:** literally, runners-of-the-woods, hunters.

l. 707. **voyageur:** the name of one of a class of men employed to transport supplies to the posts of the early trading companies, usually in canoes.

l. 713. **to braid St. Catherine's tresses:** a French saying meaning to remain single.

l. 732. **shards:** Brittle fragments of broken dishes, shells, etc.

l. 734. **devious:** winding, irregular.

ll. 733-40. **Let me essay . . . outlet.** This beautiful comparison is worthy of careful study. As the reader continues, he should observe to what degree the poet succeeds in his attempt.

l. 741. **the Beautiful River:** the Ohio, which the French called *La Belle Riviere.*

l. 749. **kith and kin:** an Old English alliterative phrase, meaning acquaintances and relatives. Other similar expressions are *bed and board, have and hold, weal and woe.* Can you add any others?

l. 750. **Acadian coast. . . . Opelousas.** See map.

l. 758. **wimpling:** rippling, like a wimple, or veil.

l. 761. **china-trees:** trees of an Asiatic variety, planted for their beauty and shade in the tropics and the southern parts of the United States.

l. 769. **tenebrous:** dark, gloomy.

l. 774. **demoniac.** Is this word aptly chosen?

l. 782. **mimosa:** also called the sensitive plant.

l. 791. **peradventure.** Now in poetic use only. Compare with *perchance* and *perhaps.*

l. 793. **colonades:** rows of columns. What are the "dark colonnades and corridors leafy"?

l. 797. **reverberant:** echoing.

l. 814. **invited.** Generally used with an object.

l. 819. **cope:** literally, a hood or head-covering.

l. 822. **pendulous:** suspended, hanging.

l. 836. **lee:** the side not exposed to the wind.

l. 842. **tholes:** pins in the side of a boat to keep the oars in place.

l. 848. **credulous:** easily deceived.

l. 854. **illusions.** What is the difference between *illusions* and *delusions?*

l. 856. **Teche; St. Maur; St. Martin.** See map.

l. 878. **Bacchantes:** women who took part in orgies in honor of Bacchus, the god of wine.

l. 890. **Yule-tide:** Christmas-tide.

l. 911. **surf.** Keeping up the figure of the sea in the preceding lines. The great prairies of the West reminded every observer of the ocean.

l. 952. **Adayes:** a town in northwestern Louisiana, a few miles from Natchitoches.

l. 953. **Ozark Mountains:** a range of hills south of the Missouri river in Missouri, Arkansas, and Oklahoma.

l. 961. **Olympus:** a mountain in Greece, fabled to be the abode of the gods.

l. 970. **ci-devant:** former.

l. 971. **patriarchal:** venerable.

l. 973. **numberless herds.** The great herds of wild cattle and horses that roamed the Southwest in early days were descended from animals brought by the Spaniards.

l. 1006. **cured,** etc. Compare l. 285.

l. 1009. **Creoles:** descendants of French or Spanish settlers of the Gulf States.

l. 1025. **Heard she the sound of the sea.** Did she actually hear it?

l. 1033. **Carthusian:** a monk of the order founded by St. Bruno in 1080.

l. 1041. **the thoughts of God in the heavens.** Compare with ll. 351-352. Which figure do you like better?

l. 1044. **Upharsin:** the last of the warning words written by the hand of the angel on the wall of Belshazzar's palace. "Daniel" v.

l. 1057. **oracular caverns:** resembling the cave at Delphi, in Greece, where the gods delivered their messages to men.

ll. 1059-61. **all the flowers . . . crystal.** Is this another of Longfellow's many Biblical references? See "Luke" vii.

l. 1075. **garrulous:** talkative, wordy.

l. 1082. **Oregon:** the Columbia, formerly so called. **Walleway.** In northwestern Oregon. **Owyhee.** In northern Nevada.

l. 1083. **Wind-River Mountains.** In Wyoming

l. 1084. **Sweet-Water.** The name of a river in Wyoming.

l. 1085. **Fontaine-que-bout:** the French name of a creek emptying into the Arkansas at Pueblo, Colorado. The phrase means "boiling spring." **sierras:** sawlike ridges of mountains.

l. 1095. **Ishmael's children.** Why is this name given to the Indians? See "Genesis" XVI.

l. 1102. **taciturn:** silent. **anchorite:** hermit.

l. 1106. **at the base of the Ozark Mountains.** Does this phrase modify *land* or *had entered?*

l. 1114. **Fata Morgana:** the mirage, which deceives travelers in the desert.

ll. 1139-1145. **Mowis and Lilinau.** These legends may be found in Schoolcraft's *Hiawatha,* which Longfellow studied.

l. 1167. **Black Robe:** a name applied to priests by the Indians.

l. 1175. **Jesuit:** a member of the religious order *The Society of Jesus,* founded in 1540 by Ignatius Loyola. The

Jesuits were extremely active in missionary work; the early history of America abounds in chronicles of their heroism and devotion.

l. 1181. **vespers:** evening songs of worship.

l. 1182. **susurrus:** whispering, murmur.

l 1184. **swarded:** grassy.

l. 1211. **mendicant:** Begging. The squirrels are compared with mendicant friars.

l. 1219. **compass-flower:** a prairie plant, the leaves of which point north and south.

l. 1226. **asphodel:** a variety of flower supposed to grow in the Elysian Fields, the abodes of the blessed. **nepenthe:** a drug, possibly opium, which the ancients used to bring forgetfulness of sorrow.

l. 1229. **wold.** open country.

l. 1240. **divers:** various; the more common form is diverse.

l. 1241. **Tents of Grace:** a settlement in Ohio, founded by the Moravians, a Protestant sect that grew up in Austria and Bohemia.

l. 1253. **sylvan:** woody, abounding in forests. What is the meaning of *Pennsylvania?*

l. 1257. **Dryads:** nymphs of the woods.

l. 1282. **abnegation of self:** self-denial.

l. 1298. **pestilence:** The yellow fever scourge of 1793, vividly desribed by Charles Brockden Brown in *Arthur Mervyn.*

l. 1299. **presaged:** foretold.

l. 1304. **brackish:** salty or distasteful.

l. 1308. **almshouse.** An attempt has been made to identify the almshouse in which Evangeline ministered with the Quaker Home, formerly on Walnut Street, between Third and Fourth. However, Samuel Longfellow, in his *Life of Henry Wadsworth Longfellow,* Vol. I, p. 73, asserts that it was rather the Pennsylvania Hospital, between Eighth and Ninth, which the poet had seen early in life, and the picture of which remained in his mind.

l. 1328. **Swedes.** The Swedish settlers had erected a church at Wicaco early in the eighteenth century.

l. 1332. **assiduous:** eager, attentive.

l. 1335. **pallets:** cots or rude beds.

ll. 1355-1356. **Hebrew . . . over.** The institution of the Feast of the Passover. See "Exodus" XII. How many references to the *Bible* occur in the poem?

l. 1390 ff. What is the effect of this return at the conclusion to the language of the beginning?